Cathe... ... a degree in Fo... ...nd Nutrition and has worked in various restaurants including the Roux Brothers' famous patisserie. She has been deputy cookery editor on *Woman's Weekly* and later cookery editor of *Home*. Catherine is now a full-time writer and food consultant to various food and lifestyle magazines and has written more than fifty cookbooks, including, *Cookies, Biscuits, Bars and Brownies* (winner in the best dessert category of the Gourmand World Awards).

Elizabeth Atkinson is passionate about food and cooking. She inspired and created many of the panini recipes in this book. A vegetarian for several years, she is now studying zoology at university and continues to write and campaign about food and animal welfare issues.

Also available fr...

Soups for Every Season
Traditional Country Preserving
Afternoon Tea
Everyday Thai Cooking
Everyday Lebanese Cooking
Everyday Curries
The Healthy Slow Cooker Cookbook
Brilliant Breadmaking in Your Bread Machine

HOW TO MAKE PERFECT PANINI

Catherine Atkinson
and Elizabeth Atkinson

Robinson
is an imprint of
Little, Brown Book Group
Carmelite House
50 Victoria Embankment
London EC4Y 0DZ

An Hachette UK Company
www.hachette.co.uk

www.littlebrown.co.uk

ROBINSON

A How To Book

ROBINSON

First published in Great Britain in 2015 by Robinson

A CIP catalogue record for this book
is available from the British Library.

ISBN 978-1-84528-577-7 (B-format paperback)
ISBN 978-1-84528-578-4 (ebook)

Typeset by Basement Press, Glaisdale.
Printed and bound by CPI Group (UK) Ltd, Croydon, CR0 4YY

How To Books are published by Constable & Robinson, a part of Little, Brown Book
Group. We welcome proposals from authors who have first-hand experience of their
subjects. Please set out the aims of your book, its target market and its suggested
contents in an email to Nikki.Read@howtobooks.co.uk

CONTENTS

INTRODUCTION

A popular choice on menus in trendy cafés, sandwich shops and busy restaurants, there's nothing quite like the flavour and aroma of freshly cooked panini hot from the press. Whether you want a quick snack, light lunch or even a main meal, a mouth-watering panini with crisp toasted bread and a hot flavoursome filling is the perfect choice.

The word 'panino' is the Italian for a small bread roll and in English we now take it to mean a hot or cold sandwich. 'Panini' is actually the plural but has become recognized as meaning a hot pressed sandwich often, but not always, with the edges unsealed, unlike a toasted sandwich. In recent years, owning a panini press has become almost as commonplace as having a toaster or blender; you no longer need to dine out to enjoy delicious fresh panini. In this book you will find all manner of classic and contemporary variations, from the simplest melted cheese to more elaborate multi-layered versions. Some of the classic well-known ones you may have already enjoyed, such as Italian Grilled Cheese and Tomato Panini (page 21) and Tuna Mayo Melts (page 26); others are newer creations, including Sticky Chilli Chicken (page 30) and Roasted Asparagus Panini with Gruyère (page 74).

If you've only got ten minutes or so to prepare and cook something to eat, turn to the Quick and Easy Panini chapter, which makes the most of fridge, store-cupboard and leftover ingredients such as sliced meat, cheeses and ready-prepared deli ingredients. When you've more time to spare, take a look at the selection of panini in the Hearty Lunches, Substantial Snacks and Suppers chapter. Many of these use the panini press as a grill to cook meats such as chicken breast and steak and a variety of vegetables. In addition to more than fifty savoury recipes, there is also a small selection of sweet recipes to satisfy those with a sweet tooth: try a rich and sticky Toffee Banana (page 56), Honeyed Fig Focaccia (page 50) or Peach Pie Panini (page 120).

All of the panini in this book can be made with bought supermarket or bakery bread, but if you are feeling especially creative, you could make your own from a selection of recipes in the bread chapter: turn to chapter four to discover how to make ciabatta, focaccia, and flatbread directly on your panini press. There are also plenty of ideas on enhancing your panini with flavoured mayonnaises, relishes, chutneys and salsas. Whatever combination of bread and filling you choose, you'll soon be making panini with flavour and flair.

FROM HUMBLE BEGINNINGS

From portable packed lunches to warm-weather picnics and dainty afternoon teas, millions of sandwiches are eaten every day. The idea is credited to John Montagu, the 4th Earl of Sandwich, who rather than interrupting his card game to eat dinner, demanded that his meat was served between two slices of bread so that he could carry on gambling and eat at the same time without getting his hands messy. Of course, Montagu didn't actually invent the first sandwich: ordinary workers had long been taking basic meals of cheese between bread to their work in the farms and fields, but he made the sandwich socially acceptable and eventually fashionable among high society.

Sandwich toasters have been around for more than a century. At their most basic, they consist of two pieces of concave cast iron which can be clamped together and held with a long handle to toast over an open campfire. The first electric toasted sandwich maker, known as the Tostwich, was invented by Charles Champion around 1920 and was patented in 1925. It was sold to restaurants and cafés rather than advertised for domestic use, and toasted sandwiches became a popular menu item. It wasn't until 1974 that Breville, an Australian company, created their Snack 'n' Sandwich toaster, with more than 400,000 selling in the first year alone. From the mid-1970s until the early 1980s, this was a must-have household appliance. The first models had a 'cut and seal' mechanism that cut the sandwich diagonally across the middle and sealed the sides. Usually made with bought white bread, buttered on the outside to give an almost 'fried' finish, it left little space inside for the filling.

The panini press is the latest trend in sandwich makers. Starting as large commercial machines which were only sold to restaurants, smaller ones soon became available for use at home and have now become a popular kitchen appliance. Although similar in some ways to the old-fashioned sandwich maker, a hinged top grill plate makes it much more versatile. And the toasted sandwich is no longer limited to supermarket sliced bread: the press allows for all manner of breads to be grilled, from the thinnest sliced bread with minimal filling, to large stuffed soft rolls. Because the edges of the sandwiches aren't sealed, you can add as much filling as you can fit into the bread.

CHOOSING A PANINI PRESS

A panini press is basically a folding appliance with two metal grill plates which are hinged together. The plates are the source of the heat and are also used to press the panini. Most panini presses have parallel ridges on the metal grill plates; these give the panini its signature grill marks. Others have a flat surface. This type will not give the browned lines that are so attractive on a panini, but will allow you to cook foods such as fried eggs and mini pancakes. Whichever you choose, look for machines that have a good-quality non-stick surface.

Panini presses are available in different sizes, colours and prices and you will need to consider these factors before you decide which type is right for you. The smallest will comfortably cook two panini, larger ones up to four, and models originally aimed at the commercial market will cook up to a dozen at a time. Most panini presses are of a sleek design in contemporary stainless steel, but you can also get them in vibrant colours or with a more traditional-looking black finish.

At the less expensive end of the market are machines intended purely for panini making, although they can easily be used for cooking other foods such as bacon, steaks and thinly sliced chicken breasts and also used for grilling vegetables. These have no controls other than a power light which indicates when the panini press is on and a ready light to show when the press has reached the correct temperature. They cook at around 180°C – perfect for toasting the outside of bread without scorching while heating through the filling. All the recipes in this book have been prepared on this type of panini press. The temperature of individual machines does vary and the cooking times given in the recipes allows for this. Check your panini after the shortest cooking time given; you can always cook it for longer if needed.

Pricier panini machines usually have temperature gauges. They won't make better panini but enable you to cook a wide range of other foods as well. The temperature can be set on maximum to sear the outside of meat but leave the inside rare, when cooking steak or fresh tuna for example, or set on a lower temperature, so that foods such as sausages can be cooked through without over-browning the outside. They will have a drip tray to catch fat and juices, either attachable or integrated, and may also have removable plates (some are even dishwasher-safe) to allow for easy cleaning. Some open out fully to allow you to use both sides as a grill and many come with a handy implement to help you clean the metal plates without scratching the non-stick surface.

CARING FOR YOUR PANINI PRESS

Your panini press will come with a leaflet or instruction booklet relevant to your particular machine. Make sure you read it! The non-stick plates are robust but can be damaged with sharp or metal implements, so always use heat-resistant plastic, wooden or silicone kitchen utensils.

Always turn the machine off and unplug when cleaning. In most cases, wiping with a wad of damp kitchen paper while the grill plates are still slightly warm is sufficient, but if your panini filling has leaked or you have cooked meat or vegetables directly on the press, use a damp cloth dipped in mildly soapy hot water and rinse off with a cloth dipped in clean water (make sure the cloths are soft and not abrasive). Be extra thorough in cleaning when you have cooked meat or fish so that you don't transfer the smell or taste to the next panini you cook.

Sometimes you may need to wipe down the panini press partway through cooking when the machine is still very hot, for example if you have cooked a steak that you are planning to serve in a hot panini. Again, unplug the machine and be careful; it's a good idea to wear oven gloves when doing this. And remember that your panini press is an electrical appliance: never submerge it in water.

TIPS FOR PANINI SUCCESS

- Balance the type of bread used with the filling: more delicately flavoured fillings such as salmon and asparagus don't work well with rustic or big, crusty bread. Similarly, strong cheeses and hot and spicy meats are less appealing served in dainty milk bread.

- Once you have chosen your bread and filling, consider how you will construct the panini. Fillings closest to the bread will be heated for longer than those in the middle. If you are making a cheese and ham sandwich, for example, you might want to place the ham between two layers of cheese, so that the cheese is soft and melted and the ham just warmed through.

- Think about how your panini will hold together; if you layer up too much meat and salad your panini may fall apart or be difficult to eat. Be less generous with these types of fillings or add cheese, mayonnaise, chutney or relish to act like 'glue' and hold other ingredients in place. You can always serve your panini with a side salad.

- When creating panini with fillings that will melt or bubble, such as cheeses, sauces, marshmallows and chocolate, leave space around the edges of the bread to prevent them oozing out during grilling. And remember that these types of fillings may become very hot, so allow your panini to cool for a minute or two before eating.

- Always preheat your panini press before adding the sandwiches. Most machines have an indicator light to show when the correct temperature has been reached.

- Watch timings carefully, checking after the shortest length of time given in the recipes; you will soon learn whether your machine cooks quickly or takes slightly longer. Take extra care when cooking panini which are made with high-fat or sugary breads, such as brioche, or are buttered on the outside, as they will cook a lot faster.

BREAD WINNERS

It's important to use good-quality bread when making panini. Ordinary sliced white or brown bread can be flattened under the lid of the panini press making it heavy or dry – although this type of bread is suited to some panini, such as Croque Monsieur, where the bread is buttered on the outside to give a crisp finish. The most popular types of bread for panini making are ciabatta, either sliced from a loaf or as rolls (ciabatta rolls are often labelled in the supermarket as 'panini') and focaccia. You will find recipes for several of those mentioned below in chapter four.

Italian breads

Ciabatta comes from northern Italy, around Lake Como. It is a light bread made with fruity olive oil; large air bubbles give it its characteristically porous, airy texture. Soft and slightly chewy on the inside, it has a thin crust that becomes deliciously crisp when grilled in a panini press. Traditionally, ciabatta is made with a *biga*, or sourdough 'starter', which adds a distinct flavour. Slice loaves on the diagonal to give larger slices or use small individual rolls.

Focaccia has a lovely soft texture and crust. It is made with a generous amount of olive oil, which flavours and moistens the bread. Extra flavourings, such as fresh rosemary, garlic or sun-dried tomatoes, are often added. It rises evenly, giving the bread a flat rather than domed top that's perfect for panini making.

French breads

Baguettes have a crisp golden crust and a chewy interior. This long thin loaf is also referred to as a 'French stick'. It contains little or no fat and is difficult to make at home as it relies on a steamy oven.

Cut into shorter lengths to use in your machine; its rounded shape can make it a bit tricky to cook, so choose slightly flattened loaves if available.

Pain de campagne is a country-style loaf with a rustic texture and a thick dark crust. It contains a small proportion of bran, which gives it an off-white colour. Pair with strong-flavoured fillings such as mature cheese and heavily spiced charcuterie.

Brioche is enriched with butter, eggs and milk and has a wonderful rich soft texture. It is traditionally made in individual moulds but use slices from a loaf for panini.

British breads

Victorian milk bread is typical of the many British breads in which milk is used as some or all of the liquid, producing a softer crumb and crust. Milk bread has an almost velvety texture and is particularly good with English cheeses and as the basis of sweet panini.

Soda bread is an everyday Irish bread, traditionally cooked in a cast-iron pan over an open fire. It is made without yeast and has a cake-like texture. It is slightly crumbly, so needs careful handling when making panini.

Granary bread has a moist texture and slightly sweet, nutty taste. The flavour comes from the process of malting the wheat, where partially germinated grains are slowly toasted. The flavour works well with both savoury fillings, especially British cheeses, and sweet ones.

Northern and Eastern European breads

Rye bread is made with the flour from rye grain. Darker and denser than most bread, with a distinctive strong flavour, it has a dense texture. Pastrami on rye is a classic American-style combination.

Bagels are chubby little rings of bread with a hole in the middle, Jewish in origin. They have a unique, chewy crust achieved through a double-cooking process – first by briefly poaching in simmering water, then baking in a hot oven.

Middle Eastern breads

Pitta bread can be round or oval, plain or flavoured, and have a pocket-like hollow in the middle. They are easily opened and filled if you warm them slightly on the panini press.

Flatbread is often used to make wraps. It can be made with flour, water and salt to produce an unleavened dough or with yeast for a lighter texture.

CONVERSION CHARTS

This book provides metric measurements for the ingredients, but
those who still prefer imperial, can use these conversions.

WEIGHT

Metric	Imperial
25g	1oz
50g	2oz
75g	3oz
100g	4oz
150g	5oz
175g	6oz
200g	7oz
225g	8oz
250g	9oz
300g	10oz
325g	11oz
350g	12oz
375g	13oz
400g	14oz
450g	1lb

LIQUID MEASURE

Metric	Imperial	US cup
5ml	1 tsp	1 tsp
15ml	1 tbsp	1 tbsp
50ml	2fl oz	3 tbsp
60ml	2½fl oz	4 tbsp
75ml	3fl oz	⅓ cup
100ml	4fl oz	scant ½ cup
125ml	4½fl oz	½ cup
150ml	5fl oz	⅔ cup
200ml	7fl oz	scant 1 cup
250ml	10fl oz	1 cup
300ml	½ pint	1¼ cups
350ml	12fl oz	1⅓ cups
450ml	¾ pint	1¾ cups
500ml	20fl oz	2 cups
600ml	1 pint	2½ cups

MEASUREMENTS

Metric	Imperial	Metric	Imperial
1cm	½in	13cm	5in
2cm	¾in	15cm	6in
4cm	1½in	18cm	7in
5cm	2in	20cm	8in
10cm	4in	25cm	10in
12cm	4½in	30cm	12in

CHAPTER ONE
QUICK AND EASY PANINI

Here you'll find a selection of the simplest panini, from a straightforward Italian Grilled Cheese and Tomato Panini to Chicken Tikka Panini and classic Croque Monsieur. These only take a few minutes to assemble and just a few more to cook, making use of fridge and store-cupboard ingredients such as sliced meats, cheeses, vegetables which don't need pre-cooking, like tomatoes and bottled grilled peppers, and ready-made sauces such as pesto.

This chapter has dozens of ideas for different fillings – you'll find not only the traditional but lots of unusual combinations that are destined to become new favourites. If you haven't used your panini press before, this is the place to start: these are panini that need minimal time and effort – fast food at its best.

Each recipe makes enough for two.

ITALIAN GRILLED CHEESE AND TOMATO PANINI (V)

A classic combination, here creamy mozzarella and tomatoes are enhanced with a scattering of fresh basil leaves that wilt and soften in the warmth, releasing their aromatic flavour.

2 home-made (page 161) or shop-bought ciabatta rolls
75g buffalo mozzarella cheese, cut into 1cm slices
1 beefsteak tomato, thinly sliced
Salt and freshly ground black pepper
6–8 fresh basil leaves

1. Heat the panini press according to the manufacturer's instructions.

2. Split each roll in half using a serrated knife. Arrange the mozzarella slices on the bottom half of each roll. Lay the tomato slices over the mozzarella.

3. Season with salt and pepper to taste, then scatter each with 3–4 basil leaves (tear into smaller pieces if the leaves are large). Add the top halves of the ciabatta rolls.

4. Put the sandwiches on the press, pull the top down and cook until the rolls are browned and crisp and the cheese is melted – 4–6 minutes, depending on how hot your machine is.

5. Carefully remove from the press and allow to cool for a minute or two before serving.

COOK'S TIPS

Instead of basil leaves, you could drizzle the tomatoes with a little basil oil (page 125) or spread thinly with 1–2 teaspoons of pesto (page 133).

Mozzarella is an Italian unripened cheese, traditionally made from water buffalo's milk but now more commonly from cow's milk. Because it has no rind, it's packed in plastic bags surrounded by water to keep it fresh. Open carefully, tipping the milky water into a small container or bowl, so that you can keep any unused mozzarella. Cover with a lid or cling film and it will keep for four to five days in the fridge.

BRIE, PEAR AND PEPPERED SALAMI PANINI

Creamy Brie is an excellent melting cheese in panini and fresh pears are the perfect contrast. Combine with a peppery salami to add lots of flavour; Italian Milano is a good choice.

4 slices home-made (page 156) or shop-bought ciabatta, about 1cm thick, cut on the diagonal
75g Brie, thinly sliced
½ firm ripe pear, quartered, cored, peeled and thinly sliced
6 thin slices (about 25g) peppered salami

1. Heat the panini press according to the manufacturer's instructions.

2. Put the bread on a chopping board and arrange the Brie on two of the slices. Top with slices of pear, followed by the salami (there's no need to season with salt or pepper as there is already plenty in the cheese and salami).

3. Top with the remaining bread slices.

4. Put the sandwiches on the press, pull the top down and cook until the panini are browned and crisp and the cheese is melted – 4–6 minutes, depending on how hot your machine is.

5. Carefully remove from the press and allow to cool for a minute or two before serving.

COOK'S TIPS

Don't be tempted to butter or oil the bread as there is plenty of fat in the salami which will moisten the panini as it warms through.

VARIATION

For a vegetarian version, use a handful of rocket leaves lightly drizzled with good olive oil instead of the salami. It will give the panini a lovely peppery flavour.

MELTING MOZZARELLA
AND CRISPY BACON

Buying ready-cooked bacon rashers means that you can prepare and serve this panini in minutes. You can, of course, cook your own bacon on your panini press first (page 100). This sandwich is especially good with shop-bought tomato chutney or home-made Cherry Tomato Salsa (page 145).

2 x 18cm lengths of baguette
3 tbsp tomato chutney
100g mozzarella cheese, thinly sliced
Freshly ground black pepper
6 rashers cooked streaky bacon

1. Heat the panini press according to the manufacturer's instructions.

2. Cut the baguettes in half lengthways using a serrated knife. Spread the chutney on the bottom halves of the baguettes.

3. Arrange half the mozzarella slices over the chutney and season to taste with freshly ground black pepper.

4. Top with the bacon, then the remaining mozzarella. Finish each sandwich with the top halves of each baguette.

5. Put the sandwiches on the press, pull the top down and cook until the baguettes are browned and crisp and the cheese is melted – 4–6 minutes, depending on how hot your machine is.

6. Carefully remove from the press and leave to cool for a minute or two before serving.

COOK'S TIP

Vacuum-packed part-baked baguettes are a useful store-cupboard standby as they usually keep for about a month after purchase and can also be frozen. If using, remove from the freezer and leave at room temperature for half an hour in advance, and allow an extra minute or two of cooking time to ensure the bread is cooked through and crisp.

CLASSIC CROQUE MONSIEUR

This iconic Parisian café snack is usually fried in butter rather than plainly toasted and sometimes includes a layer of thick bubbling béchamel sauce. It's always made with *pain de mie,* a tin-baked white bread, similar to a traditional thick-sliced British loaf. The name comes from *croquer*, meaning 'to crunch', so make sure your panini press is very hot before cooking to make the outside crisp.

4 thick slices white bread, crusts removed if preferred
25g unsalted butter, softened
1–2 tsp Dijon mustard (depending on heat of mustard and
your personal preference)
100g grated Gruyère or Emmental cheese (or four thin slices
from a packet)
2 thin slices good-quality ham
Freshly grated nutmeg or ground black pepper

1. Heat the panini press according the manufacturer's instructions.

2. Lay the bread on a chopping board and thinly spread one side of each slice with butter. Turn over and thinly spread the unbuttered sides of two of the slices with mustard, then top each with a thick sprinkling of grated cheese or a slice of cheese.

3. Top each with a slice of ham, trimming and arranging it to fit the shape of the bread if necessary, then sprinkle with the remaining cheese or another slice of cheese (so that the ham is

sandwiched between two layers of cheese), nutmeg and pepper. Finish with the remaining pieces of bread, buttered sides up.

4. Put the sandwiches on the press, pull the top down and cook until browned and crisp and the cheese is melted – 4–5 minutes, depending on how hot your machine is.

5. Carefully remove from the press and allow to cool for a minute or two. Cut each sandwich into two triangles before serving.

VARIATION

For a Croque Madame, also known as a Croque-à-Cheval in Normandy, serve poached or fried eggs on top. For poached eggs, pour about 4cm boiling water into a frying pan and add 1 tablespoon vinegar. Bring to the boil, then reduce the heat so that the water is bubbling gently. Crack an egg into a cup, then gently tip into the bubbling water. Repeat with a second egg. Cook the eggs gently for 1 minute undisturbed, then gently spoon over a little water to cook the yolks. When cooked to your liking, lift out of the water with a slotted spoon, draining off excess water.

For fried eggs, heat 1–2 tablespoons oil in a heavy-based frying pan (use just a few drops of oil in a non-stick pan). Crack the eggs into the pan one at a time. After 1 minute, spoon a little hot oil over the yolk and cook for a further minute or until the white is opaque. For a firm yolk, cook for a little longer. Use a fish slice to lift the eggs out of the pan, draining off any oil. Place one egg on top of each sandwich.

GOAT'S CHEESE, CHORIZO AND ROCKET PANINI

Use your favourite goat's cheese for this panini – soft or firm in texture, delicate or pungent – and match it to a similarly flavoured chorizo – hot and spicy or more delicately flavoured with smoked paprika. Fresh-tasting rocket, slightly wilted in the warmth, adds a final flourish.

2 squares (12 x 12cm) home-made (page 152) or shop-bought focaccia, plain or seeded
4 tsp home-made (page 140) or shop-bought tapenade
100g goat's cheese
Handful of fresh rocket leaves
8 thin slices (about 30g) chorizo

1. Heat the panini press according to the manufacturer's instructions.

2. Split the bread in half horizontally using a serrated knife. Spread the bottom half of each with 2 teaspoons tapenade.

3. Top with thin slices of firm goat's cheese, or teaspoonfuls of soft goat's cheese, then add a generous amount of rocket leaves. Arrange the chorizo slices on top.

4. Place the top halves of the bread on the chorizo.

5. Put the sandwiches on the press, pull the top down and cook until the goat's cheese has melted and the bread is golden – 3–4 minutes, depending on how hot your machine is.

6. Carefully remove from the press and leave to cool for a minute before serving.

COOK'S TIPS

Don't season with salt if you are using a black olive tapenade (which will be salty already). You may wish to add a little ground black pepper, depending on the seasoning of the chorizo used.

Shop-bought focaccia often contains extra flavouring ingredients such as rosemary or red onions, which would both work well with this panini.

If using seeded focaccia, shorten the cooking time a little as the seeds on the outside of the bread brown quickly.

PLOUGHMAN'S PANINI (V)

Crusty country bread, a wedge of mature cheese, traditionally Cheddar, a dollop of chutney and pickled onions make a classic Ploughman's. Originally eaten as a cold lunch by the ploughmen working in the fields, this combination is also delicious toasted and served hot.

100g mature Cheddar, roughly cut into small cubes (about 1cm)
4 tbsp tomato chutney or cherry tomato salsa (page 145)
1 medium pickled onion, or 2 trimmed spring onions, finely chopped
Freshly ground black pepper
4 thick slices crusty white bread

1. Heat the panini press according to the manufacturer's instructions.

2. Put the cheese, chutney and chopped pickled or spring onions in a bowl. Season with a little freshly ground black pepper, then mix well.

3. Divide the cheese mixture between two slices of bread. Top with the other two slices.

4. Put the sandwiches on the press, pull the top down and cook until the panini are browned and the cheese has melted – 4–5 minutes, depending on how hot your machine is.

5. Carefully remove from the press and allow to cool for a minute or two before serving.

COOK'S TIPS

Although you can slice the cheese and layer up the filling ingredients if you prefer, mixing them together makes the cooked panini much easier to hold and eat.

Any type of hard English cheese works well in this panini. Try Red Leicestershire or Lancashire cheese combined with an apple or fruity chutney.

FALAFEL PANINI POCKET (V)

Here, ready-made falafel are grilled on the panini press, then used to fill a pitta 'pocket' along with creamy avocado and a minted yogurt sauce, which both add moistness. You'll need to halve the falafels after cooking or the pitta bread may split in the final toasting.

6 falafel, defrosted if frozen
1 tsp mint sauce
2 tbsp Greek-style yogurt
Salt and freshly ground black pepper
1 small ripe avocado, peeled and thinly sliced
2 pitta breads (white, wholemeal or seeded)

1. Heat the panini press according to the manufacturer's instructions.

2. Add the falafel, pull the top down and cook for 1½–2 minutes or until browned and heated through.

3. While the falafels are heating, stir the mint sauce into the Greek-style yogurt and season to taste with salt and pepper. Stir in the avocado slices.

4. Remove the falafels and add the pitta breads to the press. Warm them for about 45 seconds (this will make them easy to open into pockets).

5. Remove the pittas from the press and slice an opening at one end of each, then carefully open them up into pockets. Cut the

falafels in half and insert them in the pittas together with the avocado and yogurt mixture.

6. Put the pittas on the press, pull the top down and cook for 2–3 minutes, depending on how hot your machine is, until the pittas are lightly toasted.

7. Carefully remove from the press and serve straight away.

COOK'S TIP

There are several different types of falafel available. Most contain Middle Eastern spices such as cumin and coriander, but you can also get a Moroccan variety with paprika, cinnamon and ginger, and Mediterranean ones containing lots of fresh herbs as well as spices.

ROASTED RED PEPPER AND HUMMUS PANINI (V)

Roasting red peppers enhances their sweetness and adds a delicious subtle smoky flavour. You can do this yourself (see tip below) if time allows, or simply used ready-roasted peppers from a jar. Hummus is rich in protein, vitamins and minerals, making this panini a great choice for vegetarians.

2 x 20cm flour tortillas or flatbreads (page 171)
100g home-made (page 135) or shop-bought hummus
2 roasted red pepper halves, sliced
2 tbsp Greek-style yogurt
Freshly ground black pepper

1. Heat the panini press according to the manufacturer's instructions.

2. Spoon onto and spread the hummus over one half of each tortilla or flatbread, leaving a border of about 2cm around the edge to prevent the filling oozing out during cooking.

3. Arrange the sliced peppers on top of the hummus, then dot half teaspoons of Greek yogurt over the top, dividing evenly between the two tortillas. Grind a little black pepper over the top. Fold the uncovered half of the tortilla over the filling to enclose it.

4. Put the sandwiches on the press, pull the top down and cook until they are lightly browned and crisp – 3–5 minutes, depending on how hot your machine is.

5. Carefully remove from the press and serve straight away.

COOK'S TIPS

To roast a red pepper, preheat a grill to the hottest setting. Cut the pepper in half lengthways and remove the seeds and white pith. Lightly brush the inside of the pepper with olive oil. Put the pepper halves, skin-side down, on the grill and cook for 2 minutes, then turn over and cook for a further 4–6 minutes, until the skin is charred. Place the pepper halves in a polythene bag and leave for 15 minutes or until cool enough to handle. Peel off the charred skin. Alternatively, slice the pepper and cook on the panini press (page 70).

Try a flavoured hummus rather than plain in this recipe: lemon and coriander works particularly well here. You could also use chargrilled sun-dried aubergines in oil instead of roasted red pepper, if you prefer.

GUACAMOLE, TOMATO AND BABY SPINACH BAGUETTE (V)

Guacamole is a vibrant, green-coloured spreadable dip made from avocadoes. Its rich flavour goes well with fresh tomatoes and spinach in this vegetarian panini.

2 x 18cm lengths of baguette
2 tbsp chilli or basil oil (page 124–5) or extra virgin olive oil
100g home-made (page 137) or shop-bought guacamole
6 baby plum tomatoes, halved lengthways
Salt and freshly ground black pepper
Small handful (about 10g) baby spinach leaves, long stems removed

1. Heat the panini press according to the manufacturer's instructions.

2. Cut the baguettes in half lengthways using a serrated knife and brush the cut sides with flavoured or plain olive oil. Spoon the guacamole over the bottom halves of the baguettes.

3. Arrange the baby plum tomatoes on top, gently pushing them into the guacamole, then season with a little salt and pepper.

4. Scatter with baby spinach leaves, then replace the top halves of each baguette.

5. Put the sandwiches on the press, pull the top down and cook until the baguettes are lightly browned and crisp – 3–5 minutes, depending on how hot your machine is.

6. Carefully remove from the press and serve straight away.

COOK'S TIP
Don't overcook these panini; the bread should be lightly browned and the filling just warmed with barely wilted spinach. If the centres get too hot the spinach will give out too much moisture and make the panini soggy.

PRAWN AND AVOCADO CROISSANTS

Prawn and avocado is a classic combination and here it is served with a simple seafood sauce. Grilling croissants on a panini press is a great way to warm them while retaining a crisp outer texture. Once filled they will only need to be grilled on the press for a minute or two; when served the filling should be at room temperature or the sauce will soak into the croissants.

2 large butter croissants
2 tbsp mayonnaise
2 tsp tomato ketchup
Salt and freshly ground black pepper
100g prawns, defrosted if frozen and drained on kitchen paper
1 medium ripe avocado, peeled and thinly sliced
1 tsp lemon or lime juice

1. Heat the panini press according to the manufacturer's instructions.

2. Split the croissants in half using a serrated knife, cutting almost but not quite all the way through so that the croissants are still hinged, then open up.

3. Put the croissants, cut sides down, onto the panini grill, but do not close the press. Cook for about 1 minute, or until the cut sides are lightly toasted. Remove and leave to cool for a few minutes.

4. Meanwhile, mix the mayonnaise, ketchup, salt and pepper together in a bowl. Add the prawns and mix well. Toss the avocado slices in the lemon or lime juice.

5. Spoon the prawns onto the bottom halves of the croissants, top with avocado slices then close the croissants.

6. Put the croissants on the press, pull the top down and cook for 1–2 minutes, depending on how hot your machine is, until the croissants are slightly browner and crisp.

7. Carefully remove from the press and serve straight away.

VARIATION

For chicken and avocado mayo croissants, use 150g sliced cooked chicken instead of the prawns and mix the mayonnaise with 1 teaspoon of wholegrain mustard instead of tomato ketchup.

SMOKED TROUT WRAPS WITH DILL AND HORSERADISH CRÈME FRAÎCHE

Crème fraîche subtly flavoured with horseradish is the perfect partner to flakes of tender smoked trout. Crisp cucumber and peppery watercress add texture to the filling in this satisfying light lunch or speedy supper.

1 smoked trout fillet, about 75g
4 tbsp crème fraîche
1 tsp horseradish sauce
Salt and freshly ground black pepper
2 large flour tortillas, about 45g each
25g watercress
4cm piece cucumber, unpeeled and thinly sliced

1. Remove the skin from the smoked trout and break into large flakes, discarding any bones.

2. Mix together the crème fraîche and horseradish sauce in a bowl and stir in the trout flakes. Season to taste with salt and pepper.

3. Heat the panini press according to the manufacturer's instructions.

4. Spoon the trout mixture over the tortillas and spread, leaving a border of about 2cm around the edges free of filling, then scatter over the watercress and cucumber slices. Roll up tightly to enclose the filling.

5. Put the tortillas on the press, pull the top down and cook until the wraps are lightly browned – 2–4 minutes, depending on how hot your machine is.

6. Carefully remove from the press, cut each rolled tortilla in half diagonally and serve straight away.

COOK'S TIPS

Use full-fat crème fraîche as lower-fat versions tend to separate when heated. You can use sour cream or Greek-style yogurt if you prefer.

Smoked mackerel makes a good and cheaper alternative to smoked trout. It has a much stronger flavour than trout, so you can add a little more horseradish, if liked.

SMOKED SALMON
AND CREAM CHEESE BAGEL

Probably the most famous bagel filling, this salmon and cream cheese combination is an American-Jewish classic known as 'bagels and lox' and is often eaten for Sunday brunch. Toasting the filled bagels softens the cream cheese and brings the flavours together.

2 large plain bagels
100g cream cheese
2 tsp fresh dill, finely chopped (optional)
Freshly ground black pepper
75g thinly sliced smoked salmon
Squeeze of fresh lemon juice (optional)

1. Heat the panini press according to the manufacturer's instructions.

2. Split each bagel in half using a serrated knife. Place the bagels cut-side down on the panini grill, but do not close the press. Cook for 45 seconds–1 minute or until lightly toasted, then remove and allow to cool for a minute.

3. Meanwhile, mix the cream cheese and dill, if using, together and season to taste with freshly ground black pepper.

4. Thickly spread the cream cheese mixture over the bottom halves of the bagels, then arrange the smoked salmon on top. Squeeze over a little lemon juice, if using, then replace the tops of the bagels.

5. Put the bagels on the press, pull the top down and cook until the bagels are slightly darker and warm – 2–3 minutes, depending on how hot your machine is; the cream cheese should have softened slightly, but not be melting. Serve straight away.

COOK'S TIP

'Bagels and lox' are traditionally made with plain bagels, but you can use flavoured or seeded ones if you prefer. Cook seeded ones for less time on the panini press as the seeds will brown very quickly.

TUNA MAYO MELTS

Canned tuna is a useful store-cupboard standby and makes a tasty panini on its own, but here it is paired with melted mild Cheddar cheese. Finely chopped spring onions and red pepper add colour and texture in this version, but can easily be left out, if preferred.

160g can tuna, drained
2 tbsp mayonnaise or flavoured mayonnaise (page 131)
¼ red pepper, finely chopped
2 spring onions, trimmed and finely chopped
Salt and freshly ground black pepper
4 slices ciabatta, about 1cm thick, cut on the diagonal
2 large slices (about 25g each) mild Cheddar

1. Heat the panini press according to the manufacturer's instructions.

2. Mix the tuna, mayonnaise, red pepper and spring onions together, lightly seasoning with salt and pepper to taste.

3. Put the ciabatta on a chopping board and top two slices with the tuna mixture. Place a slice of cheese on top of each.

4. Top with the remaining bread slices.

5. Put the sandwiches on the press, pull the top down and cook until the ciabatta is browned and crisp and the cheese is melted – 3–5 minutes, depending on how hot your machine is.

6. Carefully remove from the press and allow to cool for a minute before serving.

> **COOK'S TIP**
>
> Use canned salmon instead of tuna, removing any skin and bones. Mix with a lemon mayonnaise and a 2cm piece of cucumber, finely chopped instead of the red pepper and spring onions.
>
> Cutting ciabatta on the diagonal will give larger slices for panini making.

SPICY CRAB AND SALAD CLUB

A classic 'club' sandwich is made with three layers of toasted sliced bread, but here an airy ciabatta roll is used to make a lighter version. Use either ready-prepared fresh crabmeat (look for this in tubs in larger supermarkets on the deli shelves) or a well-drained can of white crabmeat.

1½ tbsp light olive or sunflower oil
2 tsp lime juice or red wine vinegar
Dash of Tabasco sauce
100g fresh crabmeat or 1 x 170g can crabmeat, drained
2 home-made (page 161) or shop-bought ciabatta rolls
1 large ripe tomato, thinly sliced
Salt and freshly ground black pepper
Small handful (about 15g) baby salad leaves

1. Put the oil and lime juice or vinegar in a small bowl. Add a dash of Tabasco sauce, then whisk together with a fork. Set aside 2 teaspoons of the dressing, then add the crab to the bowl and gently mix together, taking care not to break up the crabmeat too much.

2. Using a serrated knife, split the ciabatta rolls horizontally into three thin layers.

3. Spoon all of the crabmeat mixture onto the bottom layer of each roll, then top with the middle layer of ciabatta. Arrange the sliced tomato on top and drizzle with the reserved dressing

and a light seasoning of salt and pepper. Scatter over the salad leaves, then top with the final piece of ciabatta.

4. Put the rolls on the press, pull down the top and cook until the rolls are browned and crisp and the salad leaves beginning to wilt – 4–6 minutes, depending on how hot your machine is.

5. Carefully remove from the press and serve straight away.

STICKY CHILLI CHICKEN PANINI

This panini is delicious made with shop-bought cooked chicken, such as barbecue or char grilled style, but you can of course simply make it with leftover roasted chicken. Thinly buttering the inside of the baguette will stop the sauce soaking into the bread too much during cooking.

2 x 15cm lengths of baguette
20g butter, softened
½ tsp soy sauce
1 tsp clear honey
3 tbsp bottled sweet chilli sauce
2 spring onions, trimmed and finely chopped
200g sliced or shredded cooked chicken

1. Heat the panini press according to the manufacturer's instructions.

2. Cut the baguettes in half lengthways using a serrated knife. Thinly spread the insides with butter.

3. Put the soy sauce, honey and sweet chilli sauce in a bowl and whisk together with a fork. Stir in the spring onions, then add the chicken and mix until coated in the sauce.

4. Spoon the mixture over the bottom halves of the baguettes, then replace the top halves.

5. Put the sandwiches on the press, pull the top down and cook until the baguettes are browned and crisp – 4–6 minutes, depending on how hot your machine is.

6. Carefully remove from the press and serve straight away.

COOK'S TIP
If preferred, use ¼ chopped green pepper or a 2cm piece of cucumber, finely chopped, instead of the spring onions.

CHICKEN TIKKA PANINI

The warmth of the panini press brings out all the lovely spicy tikka flavours. The soft, slightly chewy texture of the ciabatta provides the ideal backdrop for tender chicken and crunchy toasted nuts.

2 home-made (page 161) or shop-bought ciabatta rolls
1 tbsp mayonnaise
2 tbsp Greek-style yogurt
2 tbsp mango chutney
200g cooked tikka-style chicken slices or pieces
25g roasted cashew nuts, roughly chopped
Salt and freshly ground black pepper

1. Heat the panini press according to the manufacturer's instructions.

2. Split each roll in half using a serrated knife.

3. Put the mayonnaise, yogurt and mango chutney in a bowl and stir together.

4. Add the chicken, nuts, and salt and pepper to taste. Mix well.

5. Spoon the chicken mixture over the bottom half of each roll, then place the top halves on the chicken.

6. Put the rolls on the press, pull the top down and cook until the rolls are lightly browned and crisp and the filling is slightly warmed – 4–6 minutes, depending on how hot your machine is.

7. Carefully remove from the press and serve straight away.

COOK'S TIP
Use unsalted roasted nuts if you can find them. If you can't, salted nuts are fine but reduce the quantity a little and don't season the filling with salt.

CHICKEN SATAY WRAPS

Chicken and crunchy vegetables tossed in a Thai-style peanut dressing make a delicious filling for wraps. This only takes a few minutes to make, so is perfect for a quick lunch or snack at any time.

1 tsp soft light brown sugar
2 tsp boiling water
3 tbsp crunchy peanut butter
2 tsp home-made (page 124) or shop-bought chilli oil
1 tbsp rice vinegar or cider vinegar
1 tbsp light soy sauce
200g cooked chicken slices
4cm piece cucumber, finely chopped
2 spring onions, trimmed and finely sliced
A few fresh coriander leaves (optional)
2 large flour tortillas, about 45g each

1. Put the sugar in a heatproof bowl and add the boiling water. Stir until dissolved. Add the peanut butter, chilli oil, vinegar and soy sauce and whisk together with a fork until smooth.

2. Add the chicken, cucumber and spring onions and mix together.

3. Heat the panini press according to the manufacturer's instructions.

4. Spoon the chicken mixture over the tortillas, leaving about 2cm clear of filling around the edges. Scatter over a few torn coriander leaves, if using. Roll tortilla up tightly to enclose the filling.

5. Put the tortillas on the press, pull the top down and cook until the wraps are lightly browned – 2–4 minutes, depending on how hot your machine is.

6. Carefully remove from the press, cut each rolled tortilla in half and serve straight away.

COOK'S TIP

If you don't have any chilli oil, mix 2 teaspoons peanut or sunflower oil with a small pinch of dried chilli flakes or chilli powder.

CHICKEN CAESAR SALAD PANINI

The classic Caesar salad was created in the 1920s and is named after its creator. It originally contained just lettuce, croutons and Parmesan with a creamy egg dressing, but today it is usually made with chunks or slices of cooked chicken as well.

2 home-made (page 161) or shop-bought ciabatta rolls
200g shredded roast chicken
4 tbsp Caesar dressing
25g grated Parmesan
¼ romaine lettuce, leaves torn into smaller pieces
2 firm ripe tomatoes, sliced

1. Heat the panini press according to the manufacturer's instructions.

2. Split the ciabatta rolls in half using a serrated knife

3. Put the chicken in a bowl and drizzle over 3 tablespoons of the Caesar dressing. Stir together until the chicken is lightly coated.

4. Lightly sprinkle the bottom halves of the rolls with half of the grated Parmesan. Top with the chicken followed by the lettuce.

5. Drizzle the remaining tablespoon of dressing over the lettuce, then top with the tomato slices. Sprinkle over the rest of the Parmesan and replace the tops of the rolls.

6. Put the sandwiches on the press, pull the top down and cook until lightly browned, 3–5 minutes, depending on hot your machine is.

7. Carefully remove from the press and serve straight away.

COOK'S TIP

To prepare your own Caesar dressing, mash 2 anchovies from a tin to a paste with a fork. Work in 1 small crushed garlic clove or ½ teaspoon garlic paste. Stir in 15g grated Parmesan, 3 tablespoons mayonnaise and 2 teaspoons white wine vinegar. The dressing should have the consistency of yogurt; if it is too thick, stir in a teaspoon or two of water.

TURKEY, AVOCADO
AND CRANBERRY PANINI

This is a great way to use up leftover cooked turkey. Avocado adds a creamy texture to the panini as well as moistness, and mozzarella helps bind the filling together, making it easy to eat. You can use citrus cranberry relish (page 147) or a ready-made cranberry sauce to add tangy flavour.

2 squares (12 x 12cm) home-made (page 152) or shop-bought focaccia
2 tbsp cranberry relish or sauce
200g thinly sliced cooked turkey
50g mozzarella cheese, thinly sliced
1 small ripe avocado, halved, peeled, stoned and thinly sliced
Salt and freshly ground black pepper

1. Heat the panini press according to the manufacturer's instructions.

2. Split the focaccia in half horizontally using a serrated knife. Spread a tablespoon of cranberry relish or sauce over each of the bottom halves.

3. Arrange half the turkey slices over the relish, then top with a few slices of mozzarella. Repeat with the remaining turkey and mozzarella, then finish with avocado slices.

4. Season with salt and pepper, then replace the top halves of the focaccia.

5. Put the sandwiches on the press, pull the top down and cook until lightly browned and the cheese is beginning to melt – 4–6 minutes, depending on how hot your machine is.

6. Carefully remove from the press and allow to cool for a minute or two before serving.

COOK'S TIP
This dish is also good made with Stilton or Roquefort instead of the mozzarella.

PASTRAMI ON RYE

A classic New York deli-style sandwich that usually contains a huge stack of pastrami. This version is a bit easier to eat but still contains the obligatory mustard and sour pickle. It wouldn't usually be made with butter, but this helps stop the mayonnaise from soaking into the bread as it warms.

4 x 1.5cm-thick slices dark rye bread
1 tbsp unsalted butter, softened
1 tbsp mayonnaise
2 tsp American mustard
2 sour pickles or large dill-pickled gherkins, thinly sliced
120g pack pastrami (cured beef brisket)

1. Heat the panini press according to the manufacturer's instructions.

2. Thinly spread butter on one side of each piece of rye bread and place buttered sides up on a chopping board.

3. Mix together the mayonnaise and mustard and thinly spread over two slices of the rye bread.

4. Arrange half of the pickle slices on top, then top with the pastrami slices, adding a few pickle slices between the layers of meat.

5. Top with the remaining bread slices, buttered sides down.

6. Put the sandwiches on the press, pull the top down and cook until they are crisp – 3–5 minutes, depending on how hot your machine is.

7. Carefully remove from the press and serve straight away.

COOK'S TIP
Pastrami is a cured smoked meat, usually beef, although turkey is also popular. It has a slightly dry crumbly texture and is sometimes encrusted with spices or herbs.

HOTDOG PANINI

Although heated hotdogs can be served simply in cold hotdog rolls, on a cold wintry day they are much nicer served in toasted bread with melted mustard butter. These are delicious accompanied with caramelized onions; you can buy these in a can, or make your own (page 142).

2 large hotdog rolls or home-made Cuban rolls (page 163)
4–6 frankfurters or hotdogs, depending on size
20g butter, softened
1 tbsp American-style mustard
Salt and freshly ground black pepper
Caramelized onions, tomato ketchup or shredded iceberg
lettuce and mayonnaise

1. Preheat the panini press according to the manufacturer's instructions.

2. Split each roll in half using a serrated knife. When the panini press reaches the correct temperature, put the rolls cut sides down on the press but do not close. Cook for 2–3 minutes until lightly toasted, then remove. Close the press and leave to reheat.

3. Meanwhile, put the hotdogs in a saucepan with the brine from the can or if you have bought vacuum-packed rather than canned hotdogs, with just enough hot water to cover. Gently heat for 4–5 minutes, then drain well.

4. While the hotdogs are heating, mix the butter with the mustard and a little seasoning and spread over the toasted insides of the rolls.

5. Add the hotdogs to the insides of the rolls, put the sandwiches on the press, pull the top down and cook until the outside of the rolls are lightly toasted – 3–4 minutes, depending on how hot your machine is.

6. While the rolls are toasting, gently heat the caramelized onions in the saucepan, stirring until heated through.

7. Carefully remove the hotdog rolls from the press and add caramelized onions, a squirt of tomato ketchup, or shredded iceberg lettuce and mayonnaise.

COOK'S TIPS

Don't season the butter with salt if you are using hotdogs in brine as they will be salty enough already.

As well as 'regular' frankfurters or hotdogs, look out for chicken and vegetarian frankfurters.

BLT PANINI

This classic sandwich is named after its three key ingredients: bacon, lettuce and tomato. It is always made with toasted bread; here we've suggested multigrain plus a generous amount of mayonnaise, although you can reduce this if you prefer.

4 slices multigrain bread
3–4 tbsp mayonnaise
2 leaves iceberg lettuce, torn in half, or 4 leaves Little Gem
1 large ripe tomato, sliced
8 pre-cooked rashers of bacon

1. Heat the panini press according to the manufacturer's instructions.

2. When heated, put the bread on the press but do not close. Toast one side until golden brown, about 3 minutes, depending on how hot your machine is.

3. Remove the bread and place toasted sides up on a chopping board, then close the press to allow it to reheat. Spread the mayonnaise over the toasted side of each slice.

4. Top 2 slices with half a leaf of iceberg or a leaf of Little Gem lettuce. Top with sliced tomatoes, then the rest of the lettuce. Arrange the bacon on top, then add the remaining slice of bread, toasted side down.

5. Put the sandwiches on the press, pull the top down and cook until the outsides are browned and crisp – 3–5 minutes, depending on how hot your machine is.

6. Carefully remove from the press and serve straight away.

COOK'S TIP

Sandwiching the tomato between the lettuce leaves helps keep the bacon and toast crisp during cooking. For a really crisp sandwich, spread the bread very thinly with softened butter before spreading with mayonnaise. You can add a little mustard too, if liked.

HAM AND PINEAPPLE PANINI

Smoked ham and juicy pineapple complement each other beautifully. Here the pineapple is mixed with creamy cheese to add a soft moist texture and to stop the pineapple pieces falling out of the panini.

2 home-made (page 161) or shop-bought ciabatta rolls
75g (drained weight) canned pineapple pieces in natural juice, drained
75g mascarpone or full-fat cream cheese
Freshly ground black pepper
4 thin slices good-quality smoked ham
Small handful of rocket or baby salad leaves

1. Heat the panini press according to the manufacturer's instructions.

2. Split the ciabatta rolls in half using a serrated knife.

3. Put the pineapple pieces on kitchen paper to soak up excess juice, then chop them finely. Put in a bowl with the mascarpone or cream cheese and season with black pepper. Mix well, beating the mixture for a few seconds to soften it to a spreadable consistency.

4. Spread the mixture over all four of the cut halves of the ciabatta rolls, leaving about 1cm around the edges as the cheese will soften and spread as it cooks. Top the bottom halves with the sliced ham, followed by a few leaves of rocket or baby salad leaves, then replace the top halves of the rolls.

5. Put the sandwiches on the press, pull the top down and cook until the rolls are lightly browned and the cheese soft but not melting – 3–4 minutes, depending on how hot your machine is.

6. Carefully remove from the press and serve straight away.

COOK'S TIP
Honey-roast or breaded ham slices can be used instead of smoked ham for a milder flavour.

BREAKFAST PANINI

Unlike old-fashioned sandwich makers, which sealed the edges of the toastie, the edges of a panini remain open, so a whole egg will ooze out if cooked between two slices of ordinary bread. A baguette is the ideal solution, with some of the middle, or crumb, removed to make a hollow to hold the egg.

2 x 18cm lengths of baguette
25g softened butter
2 medium eggs
Freshly ground black pepper
6 rashers cooked streaky bacon

1. Heat the panini press according to the manufacturer's instructions.

2. Cut the top third off the baguettes lengthways. Scoop out some of the bread from the middle of the bottom pieces, carefully pulling out the bread with your fingers to make a hollow measuring about 15 x 3cm and 2cm deep. Don't go right down to the crust – there should still be a good layer of bread at the bottom of the hollow.

3. Lightly butter the cut sides of the bread and the hollows. Crack an egg into each hollow and grind a little black pepper over the top.

4. Arrange the bacon on top and around the egg, then cover with the tops of the baguettes.

5. Put the sandwiches on the press, pull the top down and cook until the baguettes are browned and crisp – 5–7 minutes, depending on how hot your machine is and how well you like your eggs cooked.

6. Carefully remove from the press and serve straight away.

COOK'S TIPS

Make sure the butter is really soft and spreadable or it will be impossible to butter the insides of the hollows without tearing the bread.

Take care when placing the baguettes on the panini press as they can easily roll, causing the egg to dribble out. Close the press slowly and carefully.

If liked, cook a few sliced mushrooms on the press at the same time to serve with the panini. Toss 4 thickly sliced medium cleaned mushrooms in 2 teaspoons sunflower oil and add to the press in a single layer; you will need to turn them halfway through cooking time as the top grill won't touch them during cooking.

HONEYED FIG FOCACCIA (V)

Gentle heat brings out the delicate flavour and scent of fresh figs. With their striking bright green or purple skins and deep pink flesh, they make an attractive filling in this simple panini.

2 squares (12 x 12cm) home-made (page 152) or shop-bought plain focaccia
75g ricotta cheese
2 tsp clear honey
3 fresh figs, thinly sliced
2 tsp soft light brown sugar
¼ tsp ground ginger

1. Heat the panini press according to the manufacturer's instructions.

2. Split the bread in half horizontally using a serrated knife.

3. Mix the ricotta and honey together, beating for a few seconds until soft, then spread over the cut sides of the focaccia.

4. Arrange the fig slices on top of the ricotta on the bottom halves of the focaccia. Mix the brown sugar and ginger together and sprinkle over the fruit. Place the top halves of the focaccia, ricotta side down, on top.

5. Put the sandwiches on the press, pull the top down and cook until the focaccia is lightly browned and crisp and the filling warm – 3–4 minutes depending on how hot your machine is.

6. Carefully remove from the press and allow to cool for a minute or two before serving.

COOK'S TIP

Figs ripen very little after picking, so choose the plumpest ripe ones available; they should just yield to gentle pressure. Go by smell as well – they should be fragrant, but avoid any with a slightly sour scent. After buying, keep in the fridge and use within two days as figs are highly perishable.

BERRY BRIOCHE (V)

This makes a fantastic summer breakfast when fresh berries are plentiful and full of flavour and vitamins, but it can also be made with ready-prepared frozen berries.

2 x 2.5cm-thick slices home-made (page 165) or shop-bought brioche loaf
15g unsalted butter, softened
1 tbsp icing sugar
4 tbsp Greek-style yogurt
100g fresh or defrosted frozen berries such as raspberries and blueberries
2 tbsp maple syrup

1. Heat the panini press according to the manufacturer's instructions.

2. Thinly butter one side of each slice of brioche, then sift over the icing sugar as evenly as possible.

3. Put the brioche on the panini press, sugar side up and lower the lid until it is about 1cm away, without touching the brioche. Hold in this position for about 1 minute until the sugar starts to caramelize and turns golden; watch carefully as it darkens quickly.

4. Remove from the press and place the brioche toasted sides up on 2 serving plates.

5. Spoon the yogurt on top of the brioche, scatter with the fruit, then drizzle with maple syrup. Serve straight away.

COOK'S TIP

This is also good made with dried fruits such as apricots, dates, sour cherries and blueberries, which can be a great source of potassium and contain useful amounts of minerals such as iron as well as fibre. Chop them into small pieces, if necessary, and if time allows, soak in a little fruit juice first for an hour (or overnight in the fridge).

HOT CHOCOLATE PANINI (V)

Quick and easy to assemble, this sweet panini with a melted chocolate centre makes a satisfying snack. Use your favourite chocolate in the filling, plain, milk or white, but don't add more than is recommended in the recipe or it may ooze out and burn.

4 thick slices home-made (pages 165 and 167) or shop-bought plain or chocolate brioche or milk loaf
50g chocolate, broken into squares
1 small egg
1 tbsp full-fat milk
1 tbsp icing sugar, plus extra for dusting

1. Heat the panini press according to the manufacturer's instructions.

2. Put the bread on a chopping board and arrange the squares of chocolate over two of the slices. Top with the remaining bread slices.

3. Lightly whisk the egg with the milk and 1 tablespoon icing sugar and transfer to a wide shallow plate.

4. Dip the sandwiches one at a time in the egg mixture, turning once to completely coat both sides.

5. Put the sandwiches on the panini press, pull the top down and cook until dark golden and crisp – 3–5 minutes, depending on how hot your machine is.

6. Carefully remove from the press and dust with a little icing sugar before serving.

COOK'S TIP
Watch the panini carefully as sugary egg-coated brioche and milk loaf will brown and cook a lot faster than ordinary breads.

TOFFEE BANANA PANINI (V)

Based on the flavours of banoffee pie, this panini combines bananas and canned caramelized condensed milk in a simple sandwich. It makes a great dessert, served with unsweetened whipped cream or Greek yogurt.

4 thick slices home-made (page 165) or shop-bought brioche
1 small firm ripe banana
3 tbsp canned caramel condensed milk
1 tsp icing sugar, preferably unrefined
Unsweetened whipped cream or Greek yogurt, to serve
  (optional)

1. Heat the panini press according to the manufacturer's instructions.

2. Put the bread on a chopping board. Peel and thickly slice the banana and divide between two slices of brioche. Spoon the caramel condensed milk on top, spreading out slightly so that it goes into the gaps between the bananas; leave a gap of at least 3cm around the edges of the bread or it may ooze out during cooking and burn.

3. Top with the remaining two slices of brioche.

4. Put the sandwiches on the panini press, pull the top down and cook until dark golden and crisp – 2–3 minutes, depending on how hot your machine is.

5. Carefully remove from the press and dust with a little icing sugar before serving with whipped cream or Greek yogurt, if liked.

COOK'S TIPS

The condensed milk should only be warm when served, but make sure you check before serving.

Use unrefined icing sugar if available; it is a very pale brown colour and slightly less sweet than refined icing sugar and has a slight caramel flavour.

CHAPTER TWO
HEARTY LUNCHES, SUBSTANTIAL SNACKS AND SUPPERS

It's amazing what you can pack between slices of bread and in this chapter you'll discover all manner of savoury and a few sweet fillings. Perhaps the most obvious choices are cheese and ham, here presented in an 'Inside-out' panini and classic combinations such as Crispy Duck and Plum Sauce or Smoked Salmon with Dill. If you are looking for interesting tastes and textures and perhaps something a bit different, try a Chicken Saltimbocca or a Sloppy Joe Calzone. These are more substantial panini that may take a little more preparation time, such as pre-cooking vegetables, meats or fish for the filling.

Remember that panini don't have to be limited to two slices of bread and a single filling. Here you'll find ideas for alternative ways to present them, such as layering to make a Double-decker Panini or using puff pastry to make a Peach Pie Panini. This is a selection of ideas for those who want to expand their repertoire of recipes.

Each recipe makes enough for two.

BLUE CHEESE, PEAR
AND PECAN PANINI (V)

Roquefort is a soft, crumbly white cheese with blue-green veins and a tangy, slightly sweet flavour. It goes well with most fruit but is particularly delicious with pears. Toasted chopped pecans add both taste and a crunchy texture to this sandwich.

Small handful (about 25g) pecan nuts
15g unsalted butter
1 small firm ripe pear, quartered, peeled, cored and thickly
  sliced
2 home-made (page 161) or shop-bought ciabatta rolls
75g Roquefort cheese, thinly sliced
Freshly ground black pepper

1. Toast the nuts in a small non-stick frying pan over a medium heat for 2–3 minutes until they are just starting to colour. Tip out onto a chopping board and leave to cool for a few minutes then roughly chop.

2. Add the butter to the pan and melt over a medium heat until sizzling. Pat the pear slices dry on kitchen paper, add to the butter and cook until beginning to brown, about 3 minutes, turning once. Turn off the heat.

3. Heat the panini press according to the manufacturer's instructions.

4. Split the rolls in half using a serrated knife. Arrange a thin layer of half the cheese on the bottom half of each roll. Lightly season the pear slices with pepper, then arrange them on top of the cheese. Scatter over the nuts, then finish with the remaining cheese. Place the top halves of the rolls on the cheese.

5. Put the sandwiches on the press, pull the top down and cook until the rolls are browned and crisp and the cheese is melting – 4–6 minutes, depending on how hot your machine is.

6. Carefully remove from the press and allow to cool for a minute before serving.

COOK'S TIP
Any crumbly or creamy blue cheese can be used in this recipe – try Gorgonzola, Danish blue or Stilton for a change.

THREE CHEESE PANINI (V)

This panini is made by combining three English cheeses: flavoursome Cheddar, tangy Stilton and a soft creamy Somerset Brie. It's a fantastic way to use up leftover bits and pieces from a cheeseboard.

4 x 1.5cm-thick slices country-style or granary bread
25g mature Cheddar, thinly sliced
25g Stilton cheese, crumbled
50g Somerset Brie, thinly sliced

1. Heat the panini press according to the manufacturer's instructions.

2. Lay two slices of the bread on a chopping board and top each with thinly sliced Cheddar. Add the crumbled Stilton, then slices of brie. Top with the remaining slices of bread.

3. Put the sandwiches on the press, close the lid and cook until the bread is browned and crisp and the cheese is melted – 4–6 minutes, depending on how hot your machine is.

4. Carefully remove from the press and allow to cool for a minute or two. Cut into two triangles before serving.

COOK'S TIP

Serve with some fruity apple or tomato chutney or try a classic Waldorf salad, given a lighter twist here with the addition of yogurt in the dressing: Stir 1 tablespoon lemon mayonnaise (page 131, omitting the dill), or 1 tablespoon plain mayonnaise mixed with 1 teaspoon lemon juice, with 1 tablespoon 0% fat Greek-style yogurt and a little salt and pepper. Add 1 finely sliced stick of celery, 1 quartered, cored and diced red-skinned apple and 50g chopped walnuts, preferably toasted. Mix well. Arrange a few rocket or baby salad leaves on plates and spoon the Waldorf salad on top.

PIZZA PANINI (V)

Wraps are a great way to enclose a pizza-style filling. Choose square ones rather than round if you can find them as they will fit more easily in your panini press.

2 white or brown wraps, preferably square
2 tbsp red pesto
1 tbsp roughly chopped fresh basil or ½ tsp dried mixed herbs
100g mozzarella cheese, thinly sliced
6 baby plum tomatoes, halved
6 stoned black or green olives, sliced

1. Heat the panini press according to the manufacturer's instructions.

2. Place the wraps on a chopping board. Mix the red pesto and herbs together and spread over the wraps to within 1 cm of the edges.

3. Arrange half the cheese on one side of each wrap, leaving a space of about 2cm around the edges. Top with tomato halves, then scatter with olives. Arrange the rest of the cheese on top of the tomatoes and olives and fold over the other side of the wrap to enclose the filling.

4. Put the wraps on the press, close the lid and cook until the wraps are browned and crisp – 4–5 minutes, depending on how hot your machine is.

5. Carefully remove from the press and allow to cool for a minute or two before serving.

COOK'S TIP

Red pesto is made with sun-dried tomatoes, red peppers, pine nuts, Parmesan and olive oil. If you prefer, you can use a blend of 2 tablespoons sun-dried tomato purée and ½ teaspoon dried mixed herbs instead, or try green pesto (pesto alla Genovese).

INSIDE-OUT CHEESE AND HAM PANINI

The light texture of French baguettes is perfect for panini making, but the rounded shape can reduce the grilling area. Here the baguette is opened up, flattened and the filling sandwiched between the crusty sides of the bread.

2 x 15cm lengths of white or brown baguette
100g provolone, mozzarella or Gruyère cheese, thinly sliced
A few fresh basil leaves, torn
4 slices good-quality smoked ham
1 tsp Dijon mustard
Freshly ground black pepper

1. Heat the panini press according to the manufacturer's instructions.

2. Slice the baguettes horizontally, cutting almost but not quite all the way through (so that the bread remains 'hinged'). Open up the bread and place on a chopping board, crust side up. Lightly press down with the palm of your hand to squash and flatten the crust a little.

3. Top one crust side of each opened-up baguette with slices of cheese, then scatter over some torn basil, if using. Top with two slices of ham, trimming and arranging the ham to fit the shape of the bread if necessary. Spread the ham with a little mustard and season with freshly ground black pepper.

4. Top with the remaining slices of cheese, then fold down the tops of the baguette to enclose the filling.

5. Put the sandwiches on the press, close the lid and cook until the bread is browned and crisp and the cheese is melted – 4–5 minutes, depending on how hot your machine is.

6. Carefully remove from the press and allow to cool for a minute or two before serving.

COOK'S TIP
Provolone is an Italian cheese similar to mozzarella but with a fuller flavour. Choose a milder provolone (*dulce*) for this panini, so that the flavour of the ham isn't overpowered.

LEEK AND PARMA HAM MUFFINS

Soft English muffins work well with buttery tender leeks, rich creamy taleggio cheese and delicately flavoured Parma ham. Choose large muffins, about 10cm in diameter, for this tasty lunch or snack.

15g unsalted butter
1 leek (about 150g), trimmed and thinly sliced
1 tsp wholegrain mustard
Salt and freshly ground pepper
2 white or wholemeal English muffins
2 slices of Parma ham (about 25g in total), trimmed of fat and
  cut in half
50g taleggio cheese, thinly sliced

1. Melt the butter in a medium saucepan. Add the leeks, stir to coat in the butter, then cover the pan with a lid and cook over a medium heat for 3 minutes. Remove the lid and continue cooking for 4–5 minutes or until the leeks are very tender and any juices have evaporated. Turn off the heat and stir in the mustard. Season to taste with salt and pepper. Replace the lid to keep warm.

2. Heat the panini press according to the manufacturer's instructions.

3. Slice the muffins in half horizontally with a serrated knife. Put the muffin halves, cut sides down, onto the bottom grill of the

panini press but do not close the lid. Toast for 2–3 minutes until lightly browned, then remove from the press and place on a chopping board. Close the press and leave to reheat.

4. Spoon the leek mixture over the bottom halves of the muffins. Top with the Parma ham, arranging in loose folds, then finish with taleggio slices. Replace the tops of the muffins.

5. Put the filled muffins on the press, close the lid and cook until the muffins are browned and crisp and the cheese is melted – 4–5 minutes, depending on how hot your machine is.

6. Carefully remove from the press and allow to cool for a minute or two before serving.

COOK'S TIP

Taleggio is a semi-soft cheese from Lombardy with a strong aroma but a relatively mild, slightly tangy flavour. You can use mozzarella cheese if you prefer.

ROASTED VEGETABLE BAGUETTES (V)

Grilling vegetables adds a subtle sweetness and brings out their flavour. Here, baguettes are filled with chargrilled courgettes, peppers and red onions and a scattering of feta cheese, for a distinctly Mediterranean feel.

1 medium courgette (about 150g), thinly sliced
1 small yellow pepper, quartered lengthways, seeded and sliced
1 small red onion, thinly sliced
1 tbsp basil oil (page 125) or extra virgin olive oil
½ tsp dried Mediterranean herbs
Freshly ground black pepper
2 x 18–20cm lengths of baguette
75g feta cheese

1. Heat the panini press according to the manufacturer's instructions.

2. Put the prepared vegetables in a bowl, drizzle over the oil and mix together with your hands, to coat in oil.

3. Carefully place the vegetables on the bottom grill of the panini press (use a fork to help you, but take care not to scratch the non-stick surface). Close the press and cook for 2–4 minutes or until the vegetables are tender and slightly charred. Turn off the press, then open and return the vegetables to the bowl. Sprinkle with the dried herbs and lightly season with pepper. Wipe the panini press clean with kitchen paper.

4. Cut the baguettes in half lengthways using a serrated knife, cutting almost through but not quite, so that the two halves are still 'hinged' together. Open up the baguettes. Reheat the panini press.

5. Place the baguettes, cut sides down onto the bottom grill of the panini press but do not close the lid. Toast for 2–3 minutes until very lightly browned, then remove from the press and place on a chopping board. Close the press and allow to reheat.

6. Arrange the courgette, yellow pepper and onion slices on the bottom halves of the baguettes. Crumble over the feta cheese and close the baguettes.

7. Put the baguettes on the press, pull the top down and cook until the baguettes are browned and crisp – 4–6 minutes, depending on how hot your machine is.

8. Carefully remove from the press and serve straight away.

COOK'S TIP
For extra flavour, lightly brush some chilli or basil oil (page 124) or thinly spread some green pesto over the inside of the baguettes before filling.

PORTOBELLO MUSHROOM PANINI (V)

These large flat, dark open-capped mushrooms have a firm almost meaty texture and robust flavour. They are excellent cooked whole in the middle of panini, here topped with a little garlic butter, tender sliced onions and cheese.

2 large portobello mushrooms, 8–10cm in diameter, stems removed
1 tbsp olive oil
1 small onion, sliced
1 tsp balsamic vinegar
Salt and freshly ground black pepper
2 home-made (page 161) or shop-bought ciabatta-type rolls, preferably round in shape
15g garlic butter (page 127) or unsalted butter
50g Cheddar cheese, thinly sliced

1. Heat the panini press according to the manufacturer's instructions.

2. Brush the mushrooms with half of the oil. Put the onion slices in a small bowl with the rest of the oil and the balsamic vinegar and stir until coated.

3. Place the mushrooms and onion slices on the press, close the lid and cook for 3–5 minutes until lightly browned and soft. Turn off the press and transfer the mushrooms and onions to a plate. Season with salt and pepper.

4. Carefully wipe the panini press clean with kitchen paper, then close and reheat.

5. Split the rolls in half using a serrated knife. Thinly spread the cut sides with garlic butter.

6. Put the mushrooms, gill-side up on the bottom halves of the rolls, then add the onion slices. Top with the cheese and replace the top halves of the rolls.

7. Put the rolls on the press, close the lid and cook until the cheese has melted and the bread is golden – 4–6 minutes, depending on how hot your machine is.

8. Carefully remove from the press. Leave to cool for a minute before serving.

VARIATION

For creamy mushroom panini, thickly slice 150g chestnut mushrooms. Place in a heavy non-stick frying pan with 10g unsalted butter, 1 crushed clove garlic and 2 teaspoons chopped fresh thyme. Add 1 teaspoon water, cover and cook gently for 2-3 minutes. Uncover and cook for a further 1-2 minutes until the mushrooms are tender and the juices have evaporated. Stir in 1 tablespoon crème fraîche and season with salt and pepper. Spoon the mushrooms onto the bottom halves of the rolls. Replace the top halves and cook for 4-5 minutes, depending on how hot your machine is.

ROASTED ASPARAGUS PANINI
WITH GRUYÈRE (V)

Fine asparagus – no thicker than your little finger – can be cooked directly on the panini press. Its delicate flavour works well with Parma ham and meltingly soft Gruyère cheese.

8 thin asparagus spears, tough ends snapped off
2 tsp olive oil
Salt and freshly ground black pepper
2 squares (12 x 12cm) home-made (page 152) or shop-bought
  focaccia
2 slices of Parma ham (about 25g in total), trimmed of fat and
  cut in half
50g Gruyère, thinly sliced

1. Heat the panini press according to the manufacturer's instructions.

2. Brush the asparagus in oil and lightly season with salt and pepper. Place them on the press, arranging at right angles to the ridges on the grill (if you have a ridged rather than flat-surfaced panini press). Cook for 4–5 minutes until lightly charred and tender. Transfer to a plate.

3. Cut the focaccia in half using a serrated knife. Top the bottom half of each with a halved slice of Parma ham, arranging in loose folds. Arrange the cooked asparagus on top then the Gruyère slices and finally the remaining Parma ham. Replace the top halves of the focaccia.

4. Put the sandwiches on the press, close the lid and cook until the bread is browned and crisp and the cheese melted – 4–6 minutes, depending on how hot your machine is.

5. Carefully remove from the press and allow to cool for a minute or two before serving.

COOK'S TIPS

Sandwiching the cheese between the Parma ham stops it bubbling and oozing out of the dimpled holes in the focaccia.

This is great served with a simple tomato salad: Thinly slice two beefsteak tomatoes and arrange in a small serving dish. Whisk together 1 tablespoon basil oil (page 125) or extra virgin olive oil with 1 teaspoon lemon juice, ½ teaspoon Dijon mustard, ½ teaspoon clear honey, salt and pepper. Drizzle over the tomatoes and scatter with a handful of toasted pine nuts, if liked. Serve at room temperature.

TUSCAN BEAN PANINI (V)

The finest olive oil, fragrant fresh herbs and creamy cannellini beans are a feature of many dishes from Tuscany. Here they are used to make a purée which makes an excellent vegetarian filling for panini when combined with ripe plum tomatoes and peppery rocket leaves.

For the bean purée
2 tbsp extra virgin olive oil
1 small onion, finely chopped
1 garlic clove, peeled and crushed
400g can cannellini beans, drained and rinsed
3 tbsp crème fraîche
1 tsp chopped fresh sage or thyme
1 tbsp chopped fresh parsley
Salt and freshly ground black pepper

For the panini
2 squares (12 x 12cm) home-made rosemary or olive and
  sun-dried tomato focaccia (page 155) or shop-bought focaccia
6 baby plum tomatoes, quartered
Small handful of rocket leaves

1. To make the bean purée, heat 1 tablespoon of the oil in a small pan and cook the onion over a low heat for 10 minutes, stirring occasionally until very soft. Add the garlic and cook for a further 1–2 minutes, stirring frequently. Allow to cool for a few minutes.

2. Put the onion mixture in a food processor with the beans and the remaining oil. Blend to a fairly smooth purée. Add the crème fraîche, sage or thyme, parsley, salt and pepper and blend for a few more seconds until completely mixed. Spoon into a dish.

3. Heat the panini press according to the manufacturer's instructions.

4. Cut the focaccia in half using a serrated knife. Spoon 3–4 tablespoons of the bean purée onto the bottom halves of the bread. Arrange the tomatoes, cut-side down, and rocket leaves on top. Replace the top halves of the bread.

5. Put the sandwiches on the press and close the lid. Cook until the bread is browned and crisp – 3–4 minutes, depending on how hot your machine is.

6. Carefully remove from the press and serve straight away.

COOK'S TIPS

If you prefer a chunkier bean purée, mash the beans in a bowl with a fork or potato masher, then stir in the remaining ingredients.

Serve any remaining bean purée as a dip with vegetable crudités.

FRESH CRAB PANINI
WITH TARTARE MAYONNAISE

You can buy ready-prepared crab meat at the supermarket deli counter or in the sliced meat and prepared cooked fish aisle. It is often sold as white crabmeat – or you might like to try 'dressed crab', a mixture of white and brown crabmeat.

4 tbsp lemon-dill mayonnaise (page 131), or ready-made
mayonnaise mixed with 1 tbsp chopped fresh dill and 2 tsp
lemon juice
2 tsp capers, drained and roughly chopped
1 small gherkin (about 3cm), finely chopped
Salt and freshly ground black pepper
100g prepared crabmeat
4 slices ciabatta, about 1cm thick, cut on the diagonal

1. Put the mayonnaise, capers and gherkin in a bowl and mix together. Season to taste with salt and pepper. Add the crab and gently mix in, taking care not to break up the crab too much.

2. Heat the panini press according the manufacturer's instructions.

3. Put the bread on a chopping board and spoon the crab mixture onto two of the slices. Top with the remaining bread slices.

4. Put the sandwiches on the press, pull the top down and cook until the bread is lightly browned and crisp – 3–4 minutes, depending on how hot your machine is.

5. Carefully remove from the press and serve straight away.

COOK'S TIP

You can add a handful of baby salad leaves to the panini or serve with an avocado salad and a fruity vinaigrette dressing: Whisk together 1 tablespoon extra virgin olive oil, 2 teaspoon raspberry vinegar, 1 teaspoon finely grated orange rind, 1 teaspoon orange juice, salt and pepper in a bowl. Add 1 halved, stoned, peeled and diced firm ripe avocado and gently mix to coat in the dressing, then add 75g mixed baby salad leaves such as frisée, radicchio and lamb's lettuce and gently mix again.

FRESH TUNA PANINI
WITH WASABI MAYONNAISE

The panini press is ideal for cooking fresh tuna steaks, quickly searing the outsides while the centres remain slightly pink and juicy. Briefly marinating the steaks will help make them tender as well as adding flavour. Extra wasabi mayonnaise is added to the panini after cooking as a finishing flourish.

1 tbsp olive oil
2 tbsp soy sauce
1 tbsp rice vinegar
Pinch caster sugar
2 tuna steaks, about 150g each

For the wasabi mayonnaise panini
2 tsp wasabi paste
4 tbsp mayonnaise
1 spring onion, trimmed and finely sliced
Salt and freshly ground black pepper
2 home-made (page 161) or shop-bought ciabatta rolls
4cm piece cucumber, thinly sliced

1. Whisk together the olive oil, soy sauce, rice vinegar and sugar in a small jug. Put the tuna steaks in a shallow dish, pour over the marinade and turn the steaks to coat all over. Cover and leave at room temperature for 10 minutes or for up to 1 hour in the fridge.

2. While the tuna is marinating, make the wasabi mayonnaise: Blend the wasabi paste with a tablespoon of the mayonnaise in a small bowl. Stir in the rest of the mayonnaise and spring onions and season to taste with salt and pepper.

3. Heat the panini press according to the manufacturer's instructions.

4. Remove the tuna from the marinade and shake off the excess (or the tuna will steam rather than grill). Place the tuna on the press, close the lid and cook for 2–3 minutes; the fish should be seared on the outside, but still pink in the middle (it will cook a little more when the panini is grilled). Remove and set aside on a plate.

5. Turn off the panini press, then carefully wipe clean with kitchen paper. Reheat the press.

6. Slice the ciabatta rolls in half using a serrated knife. Place cut sides down on the press and grill for 2–3 minutes until golden brown and toasted. Remove.

7. Thinly spread the bottom halves of the rolls with some wasabi mayonnaise and arrange the cucumber slices on top. Place a cooked tuna steak on top of each, then replace the tops of the rolls.

8. Put the sandwiches on the press, pull the top down and cook until brown and crisp – 3–5 minutes, depending on how hot your machine is.

9. Carefully remove from the press and spoon the remaining wasabi mayonnaise over the tuna before serving.

COOK'S TIPS

Wasabi is similar to horseradish but grows like watercress, with its roots in water. Pale green in colour, it is usually sold as a thick paste or dried powder that you then mix with water. It's a popular ingredient in Japanese food and often served with sushi.

This dish is delicious served with a sprouted bean salad: Whisk together ¼ teaspoon ground ginger, 1 teaspoon rice vinegar, 1 teaspoon clear honey, 1½ tablespoons sunflower oil and 2 teaspoons toasted sesame seeds in a small jug. Mix 150g assorted bean and grain sprouts, such as aduki and alfalfa, with 1 small head chicory, halved lengthways and very finely sliced. Pour over the dressing and mix well. Serve at room temperature.

DOUBLE-DECKER PRAWN PANINI
WITH SPICY TOMATO SALSA

This colourful concoction has two different flavoured prawn fillings and is made with two different breads. It's ideal for those who love the healthy aspect of wholemeal bread but prefer the lighter texture and flavour of white.

For the spicy tomato salsa
200g plum tomatoes, skinned
1 small garlic clove, peeled and crushed
½ red chilli, deseeded and finely chopped, or a pinch of dried
  red chilli flakes
1 tbsp extra virgin olive oil
2 spring onions, trimmed and finely sliced

For the double-decker prawn panini
½ bunch watercress
3 tbsp mayonnaise
2 tsp lemon juice
Salt and freshly ground black pepper
150g peeled prawns, defrosted if frozen
1 tsp tomato purée
4 slices thinly cut white bread
2 slices thinly cut brown bread
25g butter, softened

1. To make the spicy tomato salsa, deseed and chop the skinned tomatoes. Put the garlic, chilli and olive oil in a bowl and whisk together with a fork. Add the tomatoes and spring onions, mix well, cover and leave at room temperature for the flavours to mingle. If making ahead, chill in the fridge and take out about 30 minutes before serving.

2. For the panini, remove any tough stalks from the watercress, then finely chop the leaves. Place in a bowl with 1½ tablespoons of the mayonnaise and 1 teaspoon lemon juice. Season with salt and black pepper, then stir in half of the prawns.

3. Blend the tomato purée with the remaining lemon juice in a bowl, then stir in the rest of the mayonnaise. Season with salt and black pepper and stir in the remaining the prawns.

4. Place the bread on a chopping board. Spread one side of the white bread and both sides of the brown bread very thinly with butter.

5. Heat the panini press according to the manufacturer's instructions.

6. Divide the watercress and prawn mixture over two slices of white bread, then top with the brown bread. Spoon the tomato purée and prawn mixture on top, dividing evenly between the two sandwiches, and top with the remaining white bread, butter-side down.

7. Put the sandwiches on the press, pull the top down and cook until the bread is brown and crisp – 4–5 minutes, depending on how hot your machine is.

8. Carefully remove from the press and cut off the crusts with a serrated knife before serving with the spicy tomato salsa.

COOK'S TIP
Make sure the prawns are well drained or they will dilute the mayonnaise too much; if necessary pat dry with kitchen paper.

TUNA NIÇOISE PANINI

This recipe is based on the classic French *salade niçoise,* omitting the green beans and with bread providing the carbohydrate content instead of new potatoes. Anchovies are included in the dressing, adding a unique salty flavour.

2 anchovy fillets from a jar or can, roughly chopped
2 tbsp olive oil
2 tsp white wine vinegar
Freshly ground black pepper
200g can tuna in olive or sunflower oil
6 black olives, halved lengthways
2 squares (12 x 12cm) of home-made (page 152) or shop-bought focaccia
Handful of baby salad leaves
2 hard-boiled eggs, peeled and sliced
2 ripe plum tomatoes, sliced

1. Mash the anchovies in a pestle and mortar or in a small bowl with a fork to a pulp, then gradually mix in the olive oil. Whisk in the vinegar and season with freshly ground black pepper.

2. Drain and flake the tuna then tip into the bowl. Add the olives and gently mix together to coat in the dressing.

3. Heat the panini press according to the manufacturer's instructions.

4. Cut the focaccia in half using a serrated knife. Put a few salad leaves on the bottom half of the focaccia, then top with layers of sliced hard-boiled eggs and plum tomatoes. Spoon the tuna and olive mixture over, then finish with the remaining salad leaves.

5. Put the sandwiches on the press, pull the top down and cook until the focaccia is browned – 3–5 minutes, depending on how hot your machine is.

6. Carefully remove from the press and serve straight away.

COOK'S TIPS

When preparing the eggs, the yolks should be semi-firm rather than hard. Use eggs at room temperature and lower on a spoon into a pan of simmering water (if using chilled eggs from the fridge, put them into cold water). Heat the water until bubbling gently again, then allow 7 minutes for medium-sized and 8 for large eggs. Eggs are easier to shell when completely cold, so plunge them into cold water immediately after cooking and change the water several times.

If liked, you can use the oil from the canned tuna to make the dressing.

SMOKED SALMON
WITH DILL CRÈME FRAÎCHE

This Swedish-style panini combines the flavours of delicate smoked salmon and aromatic dill with dark rye bread. If time allows, make one of the flavoured butters on page 127. The dill crème fraîche is added to the panini after cooking; the combination of hot and cold works particularly well here.

4cm piece cucumber, thinly sliced
Pinch of salt
4 tbsp crème fraîche
1½ tbsp chopped fresh dill
1 tsp capers, drained and roughly chopped
Freshly ground black pepper
4 x 1cm-thick slices rye bread
20g horseradish or watercress butter (page 127) or unsalted butter, softened
100g smoked salmon, thinly sliced

1. Put the cucumber slices on a plate and sprinkle with a pinch of salt. Leave for at least 10 minutes.

2. Meanwhile, mix the crème fraîche with the dill, capers and freshly ground black pepper. Chill in the fridge until needed.

3. Thinly spread one side of each slice of bread with the flavoured or unsalted butter.

4. Heat the panini press according to the manufacturer's instructions.

5. Pat the cucumber dry with kitchen paper and arrange half over two slices of buttered bread. Top with the smoked salmon, then with the rest of the cucumber. Finish with the final slice of bread, buttered side inwards.

6. Put the sandwiches on the press, pull the top down and cook for 3–4 minutes, depending on how hot your machine is.

7. Carefully remove from the press, open up the panini and spoon in the dill crème fraîche. Serve straight away.

COOK'S TIP

Salting the cucumber draws out some of the moisture and makes the cucumber crisper. Only use a small pinch of salt as the smoked salmon is already seasoned. Instead of including cucumber in the panini, you could serve this with a sweet and sour cucumber salad: Peel ½ cucumber, cut in half lengthways and remove the seeds with a teaspoon. Thinly slice, place in a sieve and sprinkle with a pinch of salt. Leave on a plate for 30 minutes to drain, then blot up any excess moisture with kitchen paper. Stir 1 tablespoon each of caster sugar, white wine vinegar and chopped fresh mint together (the sugar won't completely dissolve at this stage). Tip the cucumber into a bowl, pour over the sugar and vinegar mixture and mix well. Cover and chill for 30 minutes before serving.

SATAY-STYLE CHICKEN PANINI

Here chicken is given an Asian twist with a grated salad tossed in a peanut dressing. Allow a little extra time for both the chicken and salad ingredients to absorb the flavours of the marinade and dressing.

2 chicken breasts, about 150g each
½ tsp cornflour
1 tbsp rice wine or dry sherry
1 tbsp groundnut or sunflower oil
2 tsp light soy sauce

For the salad
2 tbsp smooth peanut butter
1 tbsp hot water
1 tsp chilli oil (page 124) or groundnut oil and a small pinch
  of red chilli flakes
1 tsp rice vinegar or cider vinegar
Pinch caster sugar
Pinch ground ginger
1 medium carrot, grated
50g white or red cabbage, finely shredded
2 spring onions, trimmed and finely sliced
2 home-made (page 171) or shop-bought flatbreads

1. Slice each chicken breast in half lengthways to make four thin pieces. Mix the cornflour with the rice wine or sherry, then whisk in the sunflower and soy sauce. Add the chicken, turning in the mixture to coat on all sides. Cover and leave to marinate at room temperature for 15 minutes or for up to 3 hours in the fridge.

2. Meanwhile, make the salad: Blend the peanut butter with the hot water, then stir in the chilli oil or groundnut oil and chilli flakes, vinegar, caster sugar and ginger. Add the carrot, cabbage and spring onions and stir to coat in the dressing. Cover and leave for at least 15 minutes, preferably a little longer; the juices from the vegetables will thin the dressing, which will be quite thick at this stage.

3. Heat the panini press according to the manufacturer's instructions.

4. Remove the chicken from the marinade, shaking off any excess and patting dry with kitchen paper if necessary (or the chicken will steam rather than grill). Place the chicken on the panini press, close the lid and cook for 4–5 minutes or until the chicken is just cooked through; it should still be moist, as it will be cooked a little longer inside the panini. Remove and set aside.

5. Turn off the panini press and carefully wipe clean with kitchen paper, then reheat.

6. Cut the chicken across the grain into thick slices. Cut each flatbread in half. Top two halves with the chicken, then with the salad. Place the second flatbread halves on top.

7. Put the filled flatbreads on the press, pull the top down and cook until the bread is slightly more browned and crisp – 3–5 minutes, depending on how hot your machine is.

8. Carefully remove from the press and serve straight away.

COOK'S TIP
If buying, make sure you use bread rather than crackers that are sometimes also labelled flatbread! As well as plain, these come in a variety of flavours: herb or garlic breads will also work well here.

SPICED CHICKEN PANINI
WITH MANGO MAYONNAISE

Although you can cook chicken on your panini press, here it is cooked in a frying pan, which allows you to stir the mixture frequently to prevent the spices burning. Team with a creamy mango mayonnaise for a sophisticated panini.

For the mango mayonnaise
100g prepared ripe mango, either fresh or from a jar (well-drained)
4 tbsp home-made (page 129) or ready-made mayonnaise
Salt and freshly ground black pepper
1 tbsp chopped fresh coriander (optional)

For the spiced chicken panini
2 skinless, boneless chicken breasts, about 170g each
1 tbsp sunflower oil
2 tsp curry paste
4 slices home-made (pages 156) or shop-bought ciabatta, about 1cm thick, cut on the diagonal
Handful mixed baby salad leaves, such as spinach and red chard

1. To make the mayonnaise, put the mango in a small food processor and process for a few seconds until roughly chopped. Add the mayonnaise and season with salt and pepper, then blend until fairly smooth. Add the coriander, if using, and briefly blend again until mixed. Spoon into a small bowl, cover and chill in the fridge until needed.

2. Cut the chicken breasts crossways into 1cm thick slices. Heat the oil in a non-stick frying pan, add the chicken and cook for 2–3 minutes until opaque, turning several times. Add the curry paste and 1 tablespoon water and cook, stirring frequently until the water has evaporated and the chicken is just cooked. Tip into a bowl and leave to cool for 5 minutes, then stir in 2 tablespoons of the mango mayonnaise.

3. Preheat the panini press according the manufacturer's instructions.

4. Put the ciabatta on a chopping board and top two slices with half of the spiced chicken. Place some baby salad leaves on top, then the rest of the chicken. Top with the remaining ciabatta slices.

5. Put the sandwiches on the press, pull the top down and cook until the ciabatta is browned and crisp, 3–5 minutes, depending on how hot your machine is.

6. Carefully remove from the press and serve straight away with the remaining mango mayonnaise.

COOK'S TIPS

If you don't have any mango, for a very simple mango mayonnaise, mix 2 tablespoons mango chutney with 4 tablespoons mayonnaise and 1 teaspoon lime or lemon juice.

Choose your favourite curry paste for this dish; they vary hugely in flavour, spiciness and heat:

Type	Main flavours	Heat
Korma	Coconut and coriander	Mild
Balti	Tomato and coriander	Medium
Biryani	Cumin and coriander	Medium
Bhuna	Tomato and tamarind	Medium
Dhanzak	Tomato and cumin	Medium
Jalfrezi	Sweet pepper and coconut	Medium
Garam Masala	Cinnamon and ginger	Hot
Madras	Cumin and chilli	Hot

CHICKEN SALTIMBOCCA

This Italian recipe – the name translates as 'jump in the mouth' –
is usually made with veal, but lean tender chicken makes a tasty
alternative. The sage wilts during cooking and the prosciutto
softens, both releasing their flavours into the chicken and bread.

1 tbsp extra virgin olive oil
1 tsp lemon juice
Salt and freshly ground black pepper
2 skinless boneless chicken breasts, about 170g each
2 home-made (page 161) or shop-bought ciabatta rolls
4 thin slices (about 50g) prosciutto or serrano ham
4 sage leaves, finely chopped

1. Whisk the oil and lemon juice together with a little salt and
    freshly ground black pepper in a small bowl. Slice the chicken
    breasts in half lengthways to make four thin fillets, add to the
    bowl and turn to coat all pieces in the marinade. Leave for 5
    minutes.

2. Heat the panini press according to the manufacturer's instructions.

3. Shake the excess marinade from the chicken (or it will steam
    rather than grill). Place the chicken on the bottom grill of the
    press, close the top and cook for 3–4 minutes or until cooked
    through and tender. Remove from the press and set aside. Turn
    off the press, wipe clean with kitchen paper, then reheat.

4. Cut the rolls in half using a serrated knife. Place a slice of prosciutto or serrano ham on the bottom half, fluting and folding it to fit. Top with the chicken, then sprinkle with chopped sage. Place the second slice of prosciutto on top and then replace the tops of the rolls.

5. Put the sandwiches on the press, pull the top down and cook until the ciabatta is browned – 4–5 minutes, depending on how hot your machine is.

6. Carefully remove from the press and serve straight away.

VARIATION

If you want to make this panini with veal, choose British 'rose veal' which comes from older calves raised on farms in association with the RSPCA 'Freedom Food'. Its name comes from the pale pink colour of the meat. Use two veal escalopes (about 150g each), cut each in half and then beat between oiled cling film or baking parchment to a thickness of around 5mm. Briefly marinade (as in chicken version) and cook on the panini press for just 2–3 minutes. Cut each escalope in half after cooking to fit the rolls and proceed as above.

CRISPY DUCK AND PLUM SAUCE

Crispy duck is often served in restaurants in steamed pancake rolls, but it is also fantastic served in plain, lightly toasted white focaccia. Use a generous amount of shredded duck and mix with the plum sauce as it will help hold the filling together.

2 squares (12 x 12cm) home-made (page 152) or shop-bought focaccia
3 tbsp sticky plum sauce
1 tsp soy sauce
150–200g shredded roasted duck
4cm piece cucumber, cut into thin matchstick pieces
2 spring onions, trimmed and cut into fine strips, about 4cm long

1. Heat the panini press according to the manufacturer's instructions.

2. Cut the focaccia in half using a serrated knife. Put cut side down onto the panini press but do not close the lid. Cook for 2–3 minutes, or until the bread is lightly toasted. Remove and close the press to reheat.

3. Meanwhile, put the plum sauce in a bowl with the soy sauce and stir together. Add the shredded duck and mix well. Spoon half the duck mixture over the bottom halves of the focaccia.

4. Top the duck with the cucumber and spring onions, sharing equally, then finish with the remaining duck. Replace the tops of the focaccia.

5. Put the sandwiches on the press, pull the top down and cook until the bread is browned and crisp – 4–5 minutes, depending on how hot your machine is.

6. Carefully remove from the press and allow to cool for a minute or two before serving.

COOK'S TIP

To prepare your own duck, put 2 duck legs, skin-side up, in a small roasting tin. Season with salt and pepper, then roast at 200°C/fan 190°C/400°F/ gas 6 for 1 hour, until the skin is a rich dark golden brown and meat comes away easily from the bone. Remove from the tin and leave until cool enough to handle, then remove the skin (you can shred this as well if you like) and shred the duck meat using two forks.

TURKEY, TOMATO AND BACON CLUB

The original club sandwich contained chicken, but turkey works just as well and this is a great way to make the most of the roast from Christmas dinner as it can be made with either breast or dark meat. Traditionally made with white bread, you can make it with seeded, brown or wholemeal, if you prefer.

4 rashers streaky bacon, rinds removed
6 slices thinly cut white bread
25g smoky tomato butter (page 128) or plain butter, softened
200g thinly sliced roasted turkey
2 tbsp citrus cranberry relish (page 147) or shop-bought
  cranberry sauce
1 ripe tomato, thinly sliced
1–2 tbsp mayonnaise (optional)
2 leaves Little Gem lettuce

1. Heat the panini press according to the manufacturer's instructions.

2. Put the bacon on the press, close the lid and cook for 3–4 minutes until well browned and crisp or done to your liking. Remove and set aside. Turn off the press and carefully wipe clean with kitchen paper. Reheat the press.

3. Put the bread on the panini press (you may have to do this in batches if you have a smaller-sized machine) but do not close the lid. Cook for 2–3 minutes until golden-brown and crisp. Remove 4 of the 6 slices of bread and set aside. Turn the other

2 slices over and cook the other side. Remove and set aside. Close the panini press and allow to reheat. Thinly butter all the toasted sides of the bread.

4. Take two slices of the bread which has been toasted on one side. Place toasted sides up and divide the turkey between them. Top with cranberry relish or sauce, then slices of tomato, followed by mayonnaise, if using. Top with the lettuce.

5. Place the bread that has been toasted and buttered on both sides on top. Arrange the bacon on the bread, breaking or cutting it to fit, then top with the remaining bread slices, toasted sides down.

6. Place the sandwiches on the panini press and gently close the lid (the sandwiches are quite tall, so do this carefully). Cook until the outsides are browned and crisp – 3–4 minutes, depending on how hot your machine is.

7. Carefully remove from the press and serve straight away, cut into two or four triangles.

COOK'S TIP
It's traditional to push a cocktail stick, or two, through the sandwich to serve, to hold everything together until you are ready to eat.

CLASSIC CUBAN

This once humble meal made from leftovers has found its way onto the lunch menu of many top-class restaurants. An authentic Cuban sandwich has both roast pork and ham, Swiss cheese, pickles and mustards and is served in a Cuban bread roll but you can substitute with ciabatta if you like.

2 Cuban rolls (page 163)
2 tbsp American-style mustard
4 thin slices (about 50g in total) Emmental cheese
50g thinly sliced roasted pork
1 finely sliced dill pickle or 2 tsp finely chopped pickled jalapeños
2 thin slices (about 50g) prosciutto or serrano ham

1. Heat the panini press according to the manufacturer's instructions.

2. Split the rolls into three horizontally using a serrated knife (so that the roll will have two layers of filling), cutting almost through but not quite, so that the rolls are still 'hinged' together.

3. Spread the mustard over the bottom layer. Add a slice of Emmental and the pork, then top with the dill pickle or jalapeños.

4. Cover with the second layer of bread and add a slice of Emmental and a slice of prosciutto or serrano ham in each roll. Fold over the top layer of the rolls.

5. Put the sandwiches on the press, pull the top down and cook until the rolls are browned and crisp and the cheese is melting, about 4–5 minutes, depending on how hot your machine is.

6. Carefully remove from the press and allow to cool for a minute or two before serving.

COOK'S TIP

For a Cuban-style salsa to serve with the panini, try this this colourful combination: Put I small crushed garlic clove, 2 teaspoons red wine vinegar, 2 tablespoons extra virgin olive oil, salt and freshly ground black pepper in a bowl and whisk together with a fork. Add ½ finely chopped red onion, mix well and leave for a few minutes (this will mellow and soften the onion). Stir in 2 chopped ripe plum tomatoes, about 100g quartered yellow cherry tomatoes and 1 peeled, stoned and diced ripe avocado. Mix well and serve at room temperature.

SLOPPY JOE CALZONE

A calzone is a folded pizza that completely encloses the filling, just like a pasty. It can easily be made on your panini press, although you do have to take care not to overfill. These contain a 'sloppy Joe' beef filling, a popular American café dish similar to a thick bolognaise sauce and often served in a bread bun.

For the Sloppy Joe filling
2 tsp olive oil
½ small red onion, finely chopped
150g lean minced beef
1 garlic clove, crushed
1 small can chopped tomatoes, about 200g
2 tsp tomato ketchup
½ beef stock cube
1 tsp chopped fresh oregano or ½ tsp dried mixed herbs
Salt and freshly ground black pepper

For the pizza dough
185g plain white flour
½ tsp salt
¾ tsp fast-action dried yeast
2 tbsp olive oil
125ml lukewarm water

1. To make the filling, heat the oil in a non-stick frying pan, add the onion and gently cook for 5 minutes, stirring frequently, until beginning to soften. Turn up the heat, add the beef and

garlic and cook for a further 5 minutes, or until the beef is well browned, stirring to break up the meat.

2. Stir in the chopped tomatoes with their juice and the tomato ketchup. Crumble over the stock cube and stir in the oregano or mixed herbs. Season with salt and pepper.

3. Bring to the boil, turn down the heat a little, cover and simmer for 15 minutes. Remove the lid and cook for a further 15 minutes, stirring occasionally until the mixture has reduced to a very thick tomato sauce; there should be very little of it left. Leave the mixture to cool.

4. While the filling is cooking and cooling, make the pizza dough: Sift the flour and salt into a large bowl and stir in the yeast. Make a hollow in the centre of the dry ingredients and add the olive oil and water. Mix to a soft, slightly sticky dough using a wooden spoon.

5. Knead the dough on a lightly floured surface for 10 minutes, until smooth and elastic. Try not to add too much flour to the surface; the dough should still be slightly sticky.

6. Place the dough in an oiled bowl, cover with cling film and leave it to rise in a warm place until doubled in size – about 1 hour.

7. When the dough is risen, turn out, lightly knead for a minute, then divide into two equal pieces. Loosely cover with cling film and leave to rest for 10 minutes.

8. Roll out each of the dough pieces to a round of about 20cm. Lightly brush the edge of each with water, then spoon an equal amount of filling onto one half of each bread round. Fold the free half of each round over the filling. Press the edges firmly together to seal, then use your fingertips to crimp the edges.

9. Heat the panini press according to the manufacturer's instructions.

10. Lift the calzone and carefully place on the bottom half of the press. Pull the top down and cook until pale golden with ridged brown grid marks – 5–6 minutes, depending on how hot your machine is. Carefully lift up the calzone and turn by 90 degrees (this will help the bread to cook more evenly and give it a chequerboard effect from the ridges on the panini press) and cook for a further 5–8 minutes, or until the bread is cooked and the filling bubbling hot.

11. Carefully remove and allow to cool for a minute or two before serving.

VARIATION

For mushroom and spinach calzone (v), steam or microwave 100g washed baby spinach leaves until just tender. Drain well and squeeze out as much excess liquid as possible. Melt 15g unsalted butter in a non-stick frying pan. Add 100g sliced chestnut mushrooms and cook for 4–5 minutes, until almost tender, then turn up the heat a little and cook until the moisture has evaporated. Add the spinach, 2 tablespoons double cream or crème fraîche, ½ teaspoon chopped fresh or ¼ teaspoon dried thyme and a large pinch of freshly grated nutmeg. Bubble for a further minute, stirring, to reduce and thicken the cream, then leave to cool. Season to taste with salt and pepper. Prepare, fill and cook calzone, as main recipe.

HOT STEAK AND STILTON SANDWICH

Here a juicy beef steak is briefly marinated, then cooked with thinly sliced and slightly charred red onions. Crumbled blue cheese melts over the steak, making this a memorable meal.

1 tbsp olive oil
1½ tsp balsamic vinegar
2 x 100g 'sandwich' or rump steaks, each about 1 cm thick
1 small red onion, thinly sliced
2 home-made (page 161) or shop-bought ciabatta rolls
1 tsp wholegrain or ½ tsp English mustard
Salt and freshly ground black pepper
50g Stilton cheese, crumbled

1. Whisk together the olive oil and balsamic vinegar in a small bowl.

2. Trim the steaks of fat or gristle, if necessary, and put on a plate. Spoon over half the oil and vinegar mixture and spread to coat the meat all over on both sides.

3. Add the onion slices to the remaining oil and vinegar mixture in the bowl and stir well to coat. Leave to marinate at room temperature for 10–20 minutes.

4. Heat the panini press according to the manufacturer's instructions.

5. Add the steaks and onions to the panini press, pull the top down and cook for 1–3 minutes, depending how well you like

your steak cooked, removing the onions after 1½ minutes when tender and lightly charred. When the steaks are cooked, remove and set aside on a plate.

6. Carefully wipe the panini press clean with damp kitchen paper (it will be very hot), then reheat. Split the rolls in half using a serrated knife. Divide the onions between the bottom halves of the rolls, top with the steaks, spread with a little mustard and season with salt and pepper to taste. Sprinkle over the Stilton cheese. Replace the tops of the rolls.

7. Put the sandwiches on the press, pull the top down and cook until the rolls are browned and the Stilton slightly melted, 3–5 minutes, depending on how hot your machine is.

8. Carefully remove from press and allow to cool for a minute or two before serving.

COOK'S TIPS

Marinating softens and mellows the onion and helps to tenderize the meat, but isn't essential if you don't have the time.

Choose steaks which are a similar shape to your rolls, so that you don't have to trim them to fit.

SAUSAGE AND MUSHROOM PANINI

Hot sausages always make a tasty sandwich, especially with the addition of a little mustard and some juicy mushrooms. Use Cuban rolls or crusty French baguettes to contain this substantial filling.

1 tsp sunflower oil
4 good-quality sausages
75g button mushrooms, thinly sliced
1 tsp soy sauce
2 Cuban rolls (page 163) or 18cm lengths of baguette
20g mustard butter (page 127), softened
Freshly ground black pepper

1. Heat the oil in a small non-stick frying pan over a medium heat. Add the sausages and turn down the heat a little. Cook, turning every now and then, for about 10 minutes, until browned all over and just cooked through. Remove the sausages and place on a chopping board. Leave to cool for a few minutes.

2. Drain most of the fat from the pan, leaving about 1 teaspoon behind. Add the mushrooms and cook, stirring occasionally, until they release their juices and are very soft – about 5 minutes. Stir in the soy sauce, then turn up the heat and cook until all the liquid has evaporated and the mushrooms are fairly dry. Turn off the heat.

3. Heat the panini press according to the manufacturer's instructions.

4. Cut the rolls in half using a serrated knife, cutting almost all the way through but not quite, so that the rolls are still hinged together. Thinly spread the inside of the rolls with mustard butter.

5. Cut the sausages in half lengthways and arrange inside the rolls. Spoon the mushrooms on top, season with freshly ground black pepper and close the rolls.

6. Put the rolls on the press, pull the top down and cook for 4–5 minutes until the rolls are browned and the filling hot.

7. Carefully remove from the press and allow to cool for a minute or two before serving.

COOK'S TIP
This is also a great way to use up leftover cold sausages. Preheat them by cooking in the panini press for 1 minute before cutting in half lengthways and following the recipe above. Wipe the press clean with kitchen paper before cooking the filled rolls.

GREEK-STYLE LAMB
WITH FETA AND MINTED CUCUMBER

This is a good way to use up leftover lean roast lamb. Slice it very thinly to make it easy to eat and bring it out of the fridge about 15 minutes before using to bring it to room temperature.

Two home-made (page 171) or shop-bought flatbreads
8 very thin slices (about 100g) roast lamb
50g feta cheese, crumbled
2–3 pitted black olives, thinly sliced

For the minted cucumber
¼ cucumber, chopped
5 tbsp Greek-style yogurt
1 tbsp chopped fresh mint
Freshly ground black pepper

1. Heat the panini press according to the manufacturer's instructions.

2. Cut each flatbread in half. Top two halves with the lamb, then scatter over the feta cheese and olives. Place a second half of flatbread on top.

3. Put the sandwiches on the press, pull the top down and cook until the bread is slightly more browned and crisp – 4–5 minutes, depending on how hot your machine is.

4. Meanwhile, mix the cucumber, yogurt and mint together. Season with pepper.

5. Carefully remove the panini from the press and serve straight away accompanied by the minted cucumber.

COOK'S TIP
Add extra flavour to the panini by lightly brushing the insides of the flatbread with basil or rosemary oil (page 125) before filling.

PULLED PORK PANINI WITH CRUNCHY NUT AND APPLE COLESLAW

Fantastically moist and tender 'pulled pork' comes from a boned pork shoulder joint cooked until really tender so that the meat can be pulled apart and shredded with two forks. You can buy it ready prepared from the deli counter or use leftovers from a roast (see tip below).

For the crunchy nut and apple coleslaw
100g white cabbage, finely shredded
1 medium carrot (about 100g) coarsely grated
1 red apple, coarsely grated
25g sultanas
2 tbsp mayonnaise
2 tbsp Greek-style yogurt
Salt and freshly ground black pepper
50g unsalted roasted nuts, roughly chopped

For the pulled pork panini
2 x squares (12 x 12cm) home-made (page 152) or shop-bought focaccia
20g mustard butter (page 127), softened
200g pulled pork
4 tbsp caramelized onions (page 142, optional)

1. For the coleslaw, mix together the cabbage, carrot, apple and sultanas in a bowl. Combine the mayonnaise and yogurt and season with salt and pepper. Add to the cabbage mixture and mix well, then cover and chill until ready to serve. Just before serving, stir in the nuts.

2. Heat the panini press according to the manufacturer's instructions.

3. Split the focaccia in half using a serrated knife and spread the insides with mustard butter. Pile the pork on the bottom halves of the bread, then top with the caramelized onions, if using. Place the top halves of the focaccia on top of the onions.

4. Put the focaccia on the press, pull the top down and cook until the bread is browned and crisp and the filling hot – 4–5 minutes, depending on how hot your machine is.

5. Carefully remove from the press and serve straight away with the coleslaw.

COOK'S TIPS

To make pulled pork to serve 4-6 with enough for leftovers for panini, place a 2kg boned pork shoulder joint (flat not rolled) in a roasting tin. Pour over 200ml cider, 200ml vegetable stock and 2 tablespoons cider or white wine vinegar. Season the joint with salt and freshly ground black pepper. Cover with baking parchment, then wrap in foil and roast at 170°C/fan 160°C/325°F/gas 3 for 3 hours. Remove the parchment and foil and roast for a further hour. When ready to serve, pull the skin back on the pork and shred the meat using two forks.

Instead of coleslaw, serve these with Pineapple Relish (page 144).

CINNAMON APPLE FRENCH TOAST (V)

This makes a really good snack or weekend brunch dish when you fancy something sweet but not too unhealthy. It works well with slices of brioche, or you can use white or multigrain bread if you prefer.

15g unsalted butter
1 apple, peeled, cored and thinly sliced
1 tbsp soft light brown sugar
1 tsp ground cinnamon
2 medium eggs
2 tsp milk
4 x 1.5cm-thick slices home-made (page 165) or shop-bought
  brioche loaf
2 tsp caster sugar

1. Melt the butter in a small non-stick frying pan. Add the apple slices, cover with a lid and cook for 2–3 minutes until beginning to soften. Remove the lid, sprinkle over the brown sugar and cook for 3–4 minutes or until the edges of the apples are beginning to brown and caramelize, turning occasionally. Turn off the heat and sprinkle over ½ teaspoon of the cinnamon. Gently mix in.

2. Heat the panini press according to the manufacturer's instructions.

3. Crack the eggs onto a shallow plate. Add the milk and lightly beat together with a fork. Carefully dip the brioche slices in the egg mixture, turning to coat both sides.

4. Put the brioche onto the panini press and pull the top down. Cook for 2–3 minutes until they are just lightly browned. Remove and place on a chopping board.

5. Arrange the apple slices on two of the brioche slices, then top with the remaining bread slices.

6. Put the sandwiches on the press, pull the top down and cook until they are browned and crisp – 3–4 minutes, depending on how hot your machine is. While they are cooking, mix the caster sugar with the remaining ½ teaspoon of cinnamon.

7. Carefully remove the toasted brioche from the press and serve sprinkled with the cinnamon sugar.

COOK'S TIP

This recipe is also delicious made with firm ripe pears when in season. Use ½ teaspoon of ground ginger and ½ teaspoon cinnamon instead of 1 teaspoon cinnamon and follow main recipe.

STRAWBERRY MALLOW PANINI (V)

Fresh strawberries combine with mini marshmallows between slices of fruit bread in this soft and sticky panini – the perfect sweet snack at any time. Serve with crème fraîche or dairy ice cream.

4 slices fruit loaf or home-made (page 167) or shop-bought milk loaf
15g softened unsalted butter
1 tbsp strawberry jam, preferably 'smooth' without bits
6 medium-sized (about 75g) strawberries, hulled and thickly sliced
15g white mini marshmallows

1. Heat the panini press according to the manufacturer's instructions.

2. Thinly butter one side of each slice of fruit or milk loaf. Place butter-side down on a chopping board, then thinly spread the unbuttered side of each with strawberry jam.

3. Top two slices of the loaf with strawberry slices, arranging them around the edge of the bread, then pile the marshmallows in the middle (as these cook, they will melt over the strawberries). Place a second slice of fruit or milk loaf on top of both.

4. Put the sandwiches on the press, pull the top down and cook until the bread is lightly browned and crisp – 2–3 minutes, depending on how hot your machine is; the marshmallows should just be melting and the strawberries slightly warm.

5. Carefully remove from the press and serve straight away.

COOK'S TIPS

Take care not to overcook or the marshmallows will ooze out of the edges; the bread should just be lightly toasted.

This is also good made with chocolate brioche (page xx)

PEACH PIE PANINI

This is a quick and easy way to bake individual fruit pies, using ready-rolled sheets of puff pastry. The pastry will not rise as much as it would in a conventional oven, but it will have a similar texture to flaky pastry and a lovely crisp, lightly browned finish.

About ½ x 320g packet ready-rolled puff pastry
½ x 400g can peach slices in natural juice or light syrup
10g unsalted butter
1 tbsp soft light brown sugar
¼ tsp ground cinnamon
2 tsp icing sugar and whipped cream or vanilla ice cream, to serve

1. Remove the pastry from the fridge and leave at room temperature for 10 minutes (this will make it less likely to crack when you unroll it).

2. Meanwhile, drain the peaches, reserving the juice or syrup. Put the butter and sugar in a small non-stick frying pan with 2 tablespoons of the juice and heat gently, stirring occasionally, until the butter has melted and the sugar has dissolved. Turn up the heat and let the mixture bubble for 2 minutes until very thick and syrupy, then turn off the heat and stir in the peach slices and cinnamon. Leave to cool while preparing the pastry.

3. Heat the panini press according to the manufacturer's instructions.

4. Unroll the pastry and cut out four 10 x 10cm squares. Put the pastry squares on the press but do not close the lid. Cook for 3–4 minutes until dark golden brown. Carefully remove from the press and place uncooked sides down on a lightly floured chopping board or baking parchment.

5. Spoon the peach mixture into the middle of two of the pastry squares (onto the cooked side), leaving a border of about 2cm clear of filling. Top with the other pastry squares, cooked sides down (so that the uncooked sides face outwards).

6. Place on the panini press, close the lid and cook for 3–4 minutes or until dark golden brown and crisp. Dust with icing sugar and serve warm with whipped cream or good-quality vanilla ice cream.

COOK'S TIP
All kinds of canned fruit, such as apricots, pears or pie filling, can be used in these fruit pies, but take care not to overfill.

CHAPTER THREE
FLAVOURINGS
AND ENHANCERS

There's more to a panini than just bread and filling: spreads, sauces, chutneys, relishes and mayonnaises all add moistness, taste and texture. Adding just a spoonful can customize your panini and add the final flourish. Of course you can buy your favourites in the supermarket, but it's fun and often less expensive to make these at home. Remember that the warmth of the panini press will bring out and intensify the flavours, so you don't have to be overgenerous. Heating may also make some of these – mayonnaises and chutneys in particular – softer or even slightly runny, so don't spread too close to the edges of the panini. Most of these recipes will make more than you need for just two panini, so store in your fridge until needed; they are unlikely to be there for long!

FLAVOURED OILS

Flavoured oils are a great way of adding both moisture and flavour to panini. They make a good alternative to butter and work especially well on drier breads with large air holes, such as ciabatta, as the oil can be lightly brushed over the cut sides of the bread to add a small amount of fat without making the panini greasy. Unlike commercially manufactured products, flavoured oils are best freshly made, so make in small quantities, keep in the fridge and use within a week or two.

RED HOT CHILLI OIL

Makes 100ml

100ml olive oil
1 tsp dried red chilli flakes
1 whole dried red chilli

1. Pour the oil into a saucepan. Add the chilli flakes and whole red chilli and gently warm for 3–4 minutes. Turn off the heat and leave to cool for 10 minutes.

2. Carefully pour the oil into a warm sterilized jar (a cold jar may crack), adding the chilli flakes and whole chilli. Cover and leave to cool.

3. Store in the fridge and use within two weeks; the oil will become hotter and more red in colour the longer it is kept.

FRESH HERB OIL

Makes 100ml

50g basil, oregano, mint or coriander
100ml olive oil

1. Bring a small pan of water to a fierce boil, add the fresh herbs and submerge in the boiling water. Blanch for just 5 seconds, then remove with a slotted spoon and plunge into a bowl of cold water. Drain well and squeeze out the water. Blot dry with kitchen paper.

2. Put the herbs in a blender or food processor with the oil and whizz for a few seconds to purée the herbs. Leave for 15 minutes.

3. Line a fine sieve with muslin or a clean unscented J-cloth and place over a jug or bowl. Pour in the herb oil and leave to strain.

4. Pour into a cold sterilized jar and keep in the fridge. Use within ten days.

COOK'S TIPS

You can also make herb oils with tougher herbs such as rosemary and thyme (but don't use tarragon as it can become bitter). Blanch in boiling water in the same way (this destroys micro-organisms), but don't blend them with the oil; add them to the oil, leave for 15 minutes, then continue from step 3.

Ideally, jars should be sterilized before use, especially if you are planning to keep oils for more than three to four days. Wash thoroughly in hot, soapy water, then turn upside to drain. The simplest way to sterilize is in a dishwasher on the hottest setting. Alternatively, half fill the clean jar with water and heat in a microwave on full power until the water has boiled for at least 1 minute. Using oven gloves, remove the jar from the microwave, carefully swirl the water inside, then pour it away. Drain upside down on a clean tea towel and allow to dry before use.

FLAVOURED BUTTERS

Great to have to hand, these are an easy way to add flavour to panini. They can either be spread very thinly or a little thicker when you want to add extra moistness to panini. Allow 10–20g of flavoured butter per panini, depending on the type and texture of the bread and richness of the filling.

Take 40g unsalted or lightly salted butter, at room temperature, and beat in a bowl with a wooden spoon until soft and creamy. Mix in any of the following flavourings:

- **Herb butter** – Add 1 tablespoon chopped fresh herbs, such as parsley, chervil, mint, dill or coriander (tarragon also works well, but isn't suitable for freezing).

- **Basil and Parmesan** – Add 1 tablespoon finely grated Parmesan (or vegetarian alternative) and 4–5 shredded basil leaves.

- **Chilli, coriander and lime** – Add the finely grated rind of ½ lime, ½ seeded and finely chopped red chilli and 1 tablespoon chopped fresh coriander.

- **Mustard or horseradish butter** – Add 1 tablespoon wholegrain mustard or 1 tablespoon creamed horseradish.

- **Garlic butter** – Add 1 crushed garlic clove.

- **Anchovy butter** – Add 3 anchovy fillets, mashed to a smooth purée, along with a dash of lemon juice.

- **Smoky tomato butter** – Add 1 teaspoon tomato purée and ¼ teaspoon ground smoked paprika.

- **Watercress butter** – Add 25g finely chopped watercress (not suitable for freezing).

- **Blue cheese butter** – Add 25g blue cheese (mash together with half the butter first, then mix with the rest).

> **COOK'S TIP**
> Most of the suggestions here can be frozen. Make double or triple the quantities given, then spoon the prepared butter onto a square of baking parchment or cling film, roll it around the butter to make a sausage shape, then twist the ends to seal. Freeze for up to a month. Slice off the amount you need and thaw at room temperature for about 40 minutes or blast in the microwave for 10 seconds.

MAYONNAISE

Home-made mayonnaise is easy to make as long as the ingredients are at room temperature and you add the oil drop by drop to prevent curdling. It can be made in a just a few minutes in a food processor or blender or you can make it by hand (see cook's tips), if you prefer.

Makes 150ml

1 large egg yolk
1 tsp lemon juice
½ tsp Dijon mustard
Salt and white pepper
150ml olive oil

1. Put the egg yolk, lemon juice, mustard, salt and pepper in a small food processor or blender and whizz for a few seconds until creamy.

2. With the machine running, pour in the oil slowly, a drop at a time. Once half the oil has been added, the rest can be poured into the machine in a slow steady stream. Continue blending until the mixture is thick and creamy.

3. Transfer to a small bowl, cover and store in the fridge until needed. Use within four days.

COOK'S TIPS

If you prefer to make the mayonnaise by hand, whisk the egg yolk, mustard and seasoning together in a small bowl. Whisk in the oil, drop by drop, until you have added about half, then whisk in the rest in a very slow, steady stream, before whisking in the lemon juice.

Choose a mild Dijon mustard; it helps the egg and oil to emulsify but the flavour should be barely noticeable in the finished mayonnaise.

If you are catering for anyone who might be susceptible to salmonella, such as pregnant women, children or elderly people, you should avoid recipes containing raw eggs. Always choose eggs with the 'lion quality' mark, which are guaranteed to have been produced to higher standards than required by UK or EU law. All 'lion quality' marked eggs are traceable and the flock will have been vaccinated against salmonella.

VARIATIONS

The following flavour variations can also be made, using ready-made bought mayonnaise if you do not wish to make your own.

- **Lemon-dill mayonnaise** – Whisk 2 tablespoons chopped fresh dill, an extra teaspoon of lemon juice and the finely grated rind of ½ lemon (preferably unwaxed) into the finished mayonnaise.
- **Red pepper mayonnaise** – Make the mayonnaise using just 100ml oil. Purée 2 halves of roasted red pepper in oil, adding 3 tablespoons of oil from the jar. Stir into the mayonnaise with ½ teaspoon ground paprika.
- **Watercress mayonnaise** – Trim the larger tough stems from a bunch of watercress, then wash, dry on kitchen paper and roughly chop. Add to the mayonnaise in the food processor with 1 teaspoon lemon juice and process briefly until finely chopped.
- **Mustard mayonnaise** – Stir 1 tablespoon wholegrain mustard into the finished mayonnaise.
- **Blue cheese mayonnaise** – Mash 50g Gorgonzola cheese with 2 tablespoons of the mayonnaise until smooth, then stir in the rest of the mayonnaise.
- **Aioli** – Add 2 crushed garlic cloves to the blender with the egg yolk when making the mayonnaise.
- **Tartare sauce** – Stir 1 tablespoon each finely chopped gherkins, capers and parsley into the finished mayonnaise.

HORSERADISH CRÈME FRAÎCHE

Less rich than mayonnaise, here crème fraîche is mixed with horseradish to provide a delicious accompaniment to thinly sliced roast beef or smoked fish such as haddock, trout or salmon. Use in panini that are only cooked for a short time, as heating too much may make the sauce runny. Don't make a large quantity of this as it will only keep for two days.

Makes 100ml

1 tbsp hot horseradish sauce (not the 'creamed' version)
100ml full-fat crème fraîche
¼ tsp freshly grated nutmeg (optional)
Salt and freshly ground black pepper

1. Blend the horseradish sauce with 2 tablespoons of the crème fraîche in a small bowl. Stir in the rest of the crème fraîche, and nutmeg, if using. Season to taste with salt and pepper.

2. Cover with cling film and keep in the fridge until needed. Use within two days of making.

COOK'S TIP

To make a seafood crème fraîche, reduce the horseradish to 1 teaspoon and add 1 teaspoon tomato purée, blending first with a little crème fraîche as main recipe.

CLASSIC PESTO

A blend of fresh basil leaves, pine nuts, Parmesan cheese and olive oil, fresh pesto is just the thing for flavouring Italian-style panini. It goes well with fish, lamb, roasted vegetables, tomatoes and cheeses such as mozzarella, feta, mild chèvre and ricotta.

Makes 150ml

50g fresh basil leaves
2 garlic cloves, peeled and roughly chopped
4 tbsp pine nuts, preferably toasted
100ml extra virgin olive oil
2 tsp lemon juice (optional)
25g freshly grated Parmesan cheese
Salt and freshly ground black pepper

1. Put the basil, garlic, pine nuts, 5 tablespoons of the oil and lemon juice, if using, in a food processor or blender. Process to a coarse paste, then stop the machine and scrape the mixture from the sides.

2. Turn the machine on again and slowly pour in the remaining oil in a thin, steady stream.

3. Transfer the mixture to a bowl and stir in the cheese. Season to taste with salt and pepper.

4. Cover and store in the fridge until needed. If you are not using it within two days of making, store in a screw-topped jar in the fridge, covered with a thin layer of olive oil; it will then keep for up to 12 days.

COOK'S TIP
Go easy on the salt as most Parmesan is already fairly salty.

VARIATIONS
- **Rocket pesto** – Replace the basil with 35g rocket and 15g fresh parsley
- **Coriander and almond pesto** – Replace the basil with fresh coriander leaves and the pine nuts with blanched almonds. Add a seeded and roughly chopped red chilli for a spicy blend.
- **Sun-dried tomato pesto** – Use 25g basil leaves and add 50g sun-dried tomatoes in oil. Replace some of the olive oil with oil from the jar (still making up the total amount of oil to 100ml).
- **Black olive pesto** – Use 25g basil leaves, 50g black olives, 25g walnut pieces, 1 clove garlic, 100ml mild olive oil, salt and freshly ground black pepper.

HUMMUS

Packed with protein, this is an excellent ingredient in vegetarian panini. It goes really well with grilled vegetables, and is also good inside tortillas; try the Roasted Red Pepper and Hummus panini on page 16. Use sparingly and grill for just long enough to brown the bread and make lightly crisp, as hummus becomes runnier when heated and may ooze out of the panini if cooked for too long.

Makes 450g

400g can chickpeas, drained and rinsed
Juice of 1 large lemon
4 tbsp light tahini paste
2 tbsp olive oil
1 garlic clove, peeled and crushed
Salt and freshly ground black pepper

1. Put the chickpeas in a food processor with the lemon juice and blend until fairly smooth.

2. Add the tahini paste, oil and garlic and blend again until smooth. Season to taste with salt and pepper.

3. Spoon into a bowl, cover and chill in the fridge until needed. Use within four days of making.

COOK'S TIP

For a creamier, slightly lighter version, stir in 2–3 tablespoons Greek yogurt. You can also add roughly chopped fresh herbs such as parsley or coriander with the tahini paste, then blend again until the herbs are finely chopped.

GUACAMOLE

When spread thickly, this avocado dip adds moistness to panini and is a great alternative to butter. It is especially good for binding ingredients together to make a panini easier to eat, or when using more delicate breads which might tear if sliced avocadoes were used.

Makes 2-3 servings

1 large avocado
2 tbsp lemon juice
2 tbsp crème fraîche
Pinch of dried chilli flakes (optional)
1 garlic clove, peeled and crushed
Dash Tabasco or Worcestershire sauce
Salt and freshly ground black pepper

1. Halve, stone and peel the avocado, reserving the stone. Mash the avocado in a bowl with the lemon juice, then stir in the remaining ingredients. Season to taste with salt and pepper.

2. Spoon into a bowl and push the avocado stone into the middle. Cover and chill in the fridge until needed. Use within two days of making.

COOK'S TIP
Storing the guacamole with the avocado stone will help keep the guacamole a vibrant green colour.

TZATZIKI

This classic Greek accompaniment is a cooling mix of cucumber, mint and yogurt. It is a great side dish to serve with hot and spicy panini and goes well with those containing roasted meat such as lamb.

Makes 2-3 servings

½ small cucumber or 1 mini cucumber
2 spring onions
100ml Greek-style yogurt
1 garlic clove, peeled and crushed (optional)
2 tbsp chopped fresh mint
Salt and freshly ground black pepper

1. Trim the ends from the cucumber and cut into 5mm dice. Place in a sieve or colander and sprinkle over a pinch of salt. Stir and place the sieve over the sink or on a plate to catch any drips. Leave for 15–30 minutes.

2. Trim the spring onions and chop finely, then stir into the yogurt with the garlic, if using, and the mint. Season to taste with freshly ground black pepper.

3. Blot the moisture from the cucumber and stir into the yogurt mixture. Cover and chill in the fridge until needed. Use within three days of making.

COOK'S TIPS

Sprinkling the cucumber with salt will draw out some of the moisture which would otherwise dilute the yogurt, but it isn't essential to do this.

Greek-style yogurt is thicker and creamier than natural plain yogurt, but you can use the latter if you prefer.

TAPENADE

This rich soft paste is readily available in supermarkets and delis, but is easy to make yourself by blending olives, capers and anchovies with a few other ingredients. It's especially good with grilled vegetables and mild creamy cheeses.

Makes 4 servings

50g can anchovy fillets, drained
75g stoned black olives
3 tbsp capers, rinsed and drained
3 tbsp olive oil
2 tbsp lemon juice
2 tbsp roughly chopped parsley (optional)
Freshly ground black pepper

1. Put the anchovy fillets in a food processor with the olives and capers. Process briefly to chop.

2. With the motor running, add the olive oil in a steady stream, followed by the lemon juice.

3. Add the parsley, if using, and season with a little black pepper. Blend until the tapenade is the consistency you prefer: slightly textured or fairly smooth.

4. Transfer to a bowl, cover and leave at room temperature for 30 minutes before using, if time allows, for the flavours to develop and mingle. If not using straight away, store in the fridge for up to one week.

COOK'S TIPS

Use a mixture of black and green olives if you prefer, and add a few sun-dried tomatoes when blending.

Spread tapenade thinly when making panini, as it is full-flavoured and fairly salty.

CARAMELIZED ONIONS

Slowly cooking onions until meltingly soft and caramelized takes a little time, but is well worth the effort. It's not worth cooking these in a smaller quantity, but they will keep in the fridge for several days (tightly covered), or can be frozen for future use.

Makes 8 servings

1½ tbsp sunflower oil
2 medium onions, thinly sliced
1 garlic clove, peeled and crushed
1 tsp soft light brown sugar

1. Heat the oil in a medium saucepan over a low heat. Add the onions, cover with a lid and cook, stirring frequently, until golden and very soft – about 30 minutes.

2. Stir in the garlic and sugar and cook for a further 5 minutes, stirring every minute.

3. Leave to cool, then transfer to a bowl and keep covered in the fridge for up to three days. Remove from the fridge about 20 minutes before using in panini to allow them to come to room temperature.

COOK'S TIP
If the onions start to stick to the bottom of the pan, stir in 1 tablespoon of water.

FRESH MANGO CHUTNEY

This quick and easy, sweet and spicy chutney is an excellent partner for grilled chicken, pork or ham. It also goes well with mature cheeses such as a strong Cheddar.

Makes 4 servings

1 large ripe mango, peeled, stoned and cut into 1cm dice
3 tbsp cider vinegar or white wine vinegar
1 tbsp soft light brown sugar
Pinch of salt

1. Put all the ingredients in a small saucepan and cook over a low heat, stirring occasionally, until the sugar has completely dissolved.

2. Turn up the heat to medium, cover with a lid and cook for 3–4 minutes or until the mango is very tender.

3. Remove the lid and cook for a further 3–4 minutes, stirring frequently, until the liquid has evaporated.

4. Leave to cool, then transfer to an airtight container, and chill in the fridge until needed. Use within five days of making.

COOK'S TIP
For chilli mango chutney, add a small pinch of dried chilli flakes to the mixture at the start of cooking.

PINEAPPLE RELISH

This simple sweet and tangy fruit relish is excellent served as an accompaniment to chicken, bacon and gammon panini. It's made using a can of crushed pineapple, so involves little preparation.

Makes 4 servings

400g can crushed pineapple in natural juice
2 tbsp soft light brown sugar
2 tbsp cider vinegar
2 spring onions, trimmed and finely chopped
1 red chilli, seeded and finely chopped
Salt and freshly ground black pepper

1. Drain the pineapple, reserving 6 tablespoons of the juice. Put the juice in a small saucepan and add the sugar and cider vinegar. Gently heat, stirring, until the sugar has dissolved.

2. Add the spring onions and chilli, bring to the boil and simmer for 3–4 minutes or until most of the liquid has evaporated and the juice is syrupy.

3. Remove from the heat and stir in the pineapple. Allow to cool, then season with salt and pepper and stir again. Tip into a bowl, cover and chill in the fridge until needed. Use within four days of making.

COOK'S TIP
If you can't find crushed pineapple, use a 400g can of pineapple rings or pieces in natural juice and chop the pineapple finely.

CHERRY TOMATO SALSA

This fresh-tasting salsa will provide moisture and flavour to any panini and is much less sweet than traditional long-life tomato chutneys. Use ripe but still firm well-flavoured cherry tomatoes for the best results.

Makes 4 servings

1 tbsp olive oil
1 shallot, very finely chopped
225g cherry tomatoes, quartered
1 tsp caster sugar
1 tsp lime or lemon juice
1 tsp finely grated orange rind
Pinch ground turmeric
1 tbsp chopped fresh coriander or parsley
Salt and freshly ground black pepper

1. Heat the oil in a saucepan over a low heat. Add the shallot and cook for 5 minutes, stirring frequently, until softened.

2. Add the tomatoes, sugar and lemon juice and cook for 3–4 minutes or until the tomatoes start to soften.

3. Stir in the lime or lemon juice, orange rind and turmeric. Cook for a further 2 minutes, then turn off the heat.

4. Stir in the coriander or parsley and season to taste with salt and pepper. Leave to cool, then spoon into a bowl, cover with cling

film and store in the fridge until needed. Use within three days of making.

COOK'S TIP
Use baby plum tomatoes or a mixture of red and yellow cherry tomatoes if you prefer.

CITRUS CRANBERRY RELISH

This relish has a lovely vibrant colour and is just the right ingredient to jazz up leftover roast turkey, chicken or ham. It's less sweet than commercially made versions and can be frozen, so it's worth making double the quantity when cranberries are in season.

Makes 4-6 servings

100g fresh cranberries, rinsed
3 tbsp orange juice or water
3 tbsp caster sugar
2 tsp finely grated orange rind
1 tsp finely grated lime rind (optional)

1. Put the cranberries and orange juice or water in a small saucepan, cover with a lid and bring to the boil over a medium heat. Lower the heat and simmer, stirring occasionally, for 3–4 minutes or until the cranberries start to pop.

2. Add the sugar and citrus rind and stir until the sugar has dissolved. Simmer for a further 3–4 minutes uncovered.

3. Leave to cool, then transfer to an airtight container or bowl covered with cling film and keep in the fridge until needed. Use within one week of making.

COOK'S TIPS

Use unwaxed citrus fruit, if possible, or wash the fruit well in hot water and dry before grating the rind.

For a spiced cranberry sauce, add ¼ teaspoon each ground cinnamon and ginger and a tiny pinch of freshly grated nutmeg with the sugar and citrus rind.

BABA GANOUSH

Middle-Eastern in origin, this aubergine spread is wonderful for vegetarian panini when combined with slivers of sun-dried tomatoes and some crumbled feta cheese.

Makes 4-6 servings

1 medium aubergine
3 tbsp olive oil
2 cloves garlic, roughly chopped
Juice of 1 medium lemon
2 tbsp tahini
3 tbsp water
2 tbsp roughly chopped fresh parsley
Salt and freshly ground black pepper

1. Trim the aubergine, then cut into 1cm thick slices. Lightly brush both sides with the oil.

2. Heat the panini press according to the manufacturer's instructions.

3. Arrange the aubergine slices on the press (it may be necessary to cook in two or more batches), close the lid and cook for 4–5 minutes, depending on how hot your press is, until the aubergine is very well cooked and tender. Remove from the press and set aside to cool for a few minutes.

4. Put the aubergine slices, garlic, lemon juice, tahini and water in a food processor and process until finely chopped. Scrape down the mixture from the sides, add the parsley, then process again until fairly smooth. Season to taste with salt and pepper.

5. Transfer to a bowl, cover with cling film and chill in the fridge until needed. Use within five days of making.

COOK'S TIP

The aubergine can be roasted in the oven if you prefer, and the skin removed to make a creamy-coloured spread: Place the whole aubergine on a baking tray and prick a few times with a fork. Roast at 200°C/fan 190°C/400°F/gas 6 for 20 minutes, turning halfway through cooking time, until it is blackened and wrinkled and soft when gently squeezed. Remove and leave until cool enough to handle, then peel the skin from the aubergine.

CHAPTER FOUR
BREADS

Bread is a crucial component of any panini, whether it's sliced, stuffed, folded or wrapped. A well-flavoured and good-quality loaf, roll or flatbread makes a huge difference to the finished result. Crusty or soft, airy or dense, white, brown, seeded or flavoured, it's vital to match your bread to the filling of your choice. While all of the recipes in this book can be made with shop-bought bread, you may also welcome the opportunity to make your own – there's nothing like the flavour and aroma of fresh home-baked bread. The benefits are obvious: not only do you get the freshest bread but you know exactly what's in it and can create loaves or rolls to suit your personal preferences. Most of the recipes here are easy to make and don't require any special equipment. The chapter includes a recipe for a quick and easy non-yeasted bread and another for flatbread that is cooked on the panini press.

FOCACCIA

This Italian bread dates from Roman times, when it was cooked in the hot ashes of the fire, *focus* being the Latin for 'hearth'. Perfect for panini making, focaccia rises evenly rather than as a domed loaf. The dough is enriched with olive oil and a little more is drizzled over the dimpled top before baking, making the bread soft and moist. It can be flavoured in many different ways, typically with rosemary, olives or sun-dried tomatoes.

Makes six 12 x 12cm squares

475g strong white flour, plus extra for dusting
1½ tsp salt
1 tsp fast-action dried yeast
300ml lukewarm water
5 tbsp olive oil, plus extra for oiling
Sea salt flakes (optional)

1. Sift the flour and salt into a large bowl and stir in the yeast. Make a hollow in the middle of the dry ingredients. Add the water and 3 tablespoons of the oil to the hollow and mix to a soft dough using a wooden spoon.

2. Turn out the dough onto a lightly floured work surface and knead for 10 minutes, until smooth and elastic. Place in an oiled bowl, cover with a clean tea towel and leave to rise in a warm place for 1½–2 hours or until doubled in size.

3. Lightly oil a large baking tray measuring about 35 x 25cm. Turn out the risen dough and punch down to deflate. Roll out the dough to a rectangle, about the size of the baking tray, then carefully place it on the tray and ease out the dough towards the edges.

4. Cover loosely with oiled cling film and leave in a warm place to rise for 30 minutes or until well risen.

5. Using the end of a wooden spoon dipped in flour, make deep dimples all over the dough right through to the bottom of the tray. Drizzle or brush the top with the remaining 2 tablespoons olive oil.

6. Sprinkle with sea salt flakes, if using. Re-cover the focaccia with the cling film and leave to rise for a further 5 minutes.

7. Preheat the oven to 200°C/fan 190°C/400°F/gas 6.

8. If you have a water spray, spray the top of the loaf with water (this will help keep the crust soft). Bake for 20–25 minutes until firm and golden (don't overcook; the crust should be light brown, not dark, in colour). Transfer to a wire rack and leave to cool.

COOK'S TIPS

To make the dough in a bread machine, pour the water and 3 tablespoons of the oil into the bread pan. Add the flour, then put the salt and yeast in separate corners of the pan. Fit the pan into the bread machine, shut the lid and set to the dough setting. Press start. Complete the focaccia following the recipe from step 3.

The focaccia can also be cooked as a round which can then be cut into triangles for panini making: Roll out the dough to a 25cm round. Grease a 28cm metal flan ring and place on a lightly greased baking sheet. Put the dough in the middle, then push the dough to the edges using your fingertips. If you haven't got a flan ring, simply roll the dough into a 25cm round and transfer to the baking sheet. Prove and bake as main recipe.

VARIATIONS

- **Rosemary focaccia** – Knead 1 tablespoon roughly chopped fresh rosemary leaves into the dough before shaping. When risen, drizzle or brush with olive oil as before, then poke about 12 tiny sprigs of rosemary randomly into the dough.
- **Olive and sun-dried tomato focaccia** – Reduce the salt to 1 teaspoon. Drain 50g sun-dried tomatoes in oil and roughly chop with 50g black or green olives. Knead into the dough before shaping. You can use the oil from the sun-dried tomatoes in place of the olive oil in the dough, if liked, to add extra flavour.
- **Seeded focaccia** – Toast 25g sunflower seeds, 25g pumpkin seeds and 2 tablespoons sesame seeds in a small non-stick frying pan over a medium heat for 2–3 minutes or until they smell fragrant and nutty. Allow to cool a little before kneading into the dough and then shaping.

COUNTRY-STYLE CIABATTA

Ciabatta means 'slipper' in Italian and describes these flattish oval loaves, which have a lovely light texture and crisp crust. This polenta-enriched version is more like the country-style ciabatta made in Italian homes than those found at the supermarket. It does involve a lot of waiting time as the dough is proved in the refrigerator to allow the flavour to develop, but needs little kneading.

Makes 2 x 450g loaves

650g strong white bread flour
1 tsp caster sugar
1½ tsp salt
225g polenta or cornmeal
1½ tsp fast-action dried yeast
450ml lukewarm water
1 tbsp olive oil, plus extra for oiling

1. Sift the flour, sugar and salt into a large bowl and stir in the polenta and yeast. Make a hollow in the middle of the dry ingredients. Add the water and oil to the hollow and mix to a soft dough using a wooden spoon. Place in an oiled bowl, cover with cling film and leave to rise for 2–3 hours.

2. Turn out the dough onto a lightly floured surface and knead for 2–3 minutes until smooth. Divide in half and place each piece in a tied large oiled polythene bag or in bowls covered with cling film. Chill in the fridge for 24 hours.

3. The following day, remove the dough from the fridge and leave
for 1 hour to come to room temperature. Knead on a lightly
floured surface and shape each piece into a long oval. Place on
baking sheets, cover with oiled cling film and leave to rise for
about 45 minutes, until doubled in size.

4. Place a small roasting tin half-filled with hot water in the
bottom of the oven and heat oven to 240°C/fan 220°C/
475°F/gas 9.

5. Carefully remove the cling film and bake for 10 minutes, then
lower the oven temperature to 190°C/fan 180°C/375°F/gas 5.
Bake for a further 15–20 minutes or until dark golden and
hollow-sounding when tapped.

6. Transfer the loaves to a wire rack and leave to cool.

COOK'S TIP

For olive and oregano ciabatta, reduce the salt in the dough to
1 teaspoon and add 1½ teaspoons dried oregano with the flour.
Knead 50g chopped stoned black olives into the dough after the
second rising and before shaping into loaves.

CLASSIC CIABATTA

This is a traditional ciabatta recipe made with a sourdough starter which gives the bread a distinctive, slightly acidic flavour and a more aerated texture. The recipe used here contains dried yeast, although traditionally it would have been made without commercial yeast, and the flour and water mixture would have relied on natural yeasts present in the air and on the flour. When you have used some of your starter, you can 'feed' and replenish it; providing you do this, it should keep indefinitely.

Makes 2 x 350g loaves

For the sourdough starter
250g strong white bread flour
2 tsp fast-action dried yeast
300ml water

For the ciabatta
350g strong white bread flour
1½ tsp salt
½ tsp fast-action dried yeast
150ml lukewarm water
2 tbsp olive oil, plus extra for oiling
300ml sourdough starter

1. To make the sourdough starter, put the flour and yeast in a large bowl and stir together. Make a hollow in the middle and add the water. Gradually blend in with a wooden spoon or whisk to make a thick batter.

2. Cover with a clean tea towel or piece of muslin and leave undisturbed in a cool room, away from direct sunlight for three to five days to ferment. The batter is ready when it is frothy and has a pleasantly sour smell. Cover the bowl with cling film and store in the fridge.

3. Before using the starter, remove from the fridge and leave for about 30 minutes to reach room temperature. Stir the batter, then remove the amount required with a ladle.

4. If you want to continue using the starter for future breads, replenish by the amount you have removed (you need to do this at least every two weeks). For example, if you have used 300ml, you will need to add 150ml water and 150g flour. Let this ferment at room temperature as before for 24 hours, then store in the fridge.

5. To make the ciabatta, sift the flour and salt into a bowl and stir in the yeast. Make a hollow in the middle of the dry ingredients and pour in the water, olive oil and sourdough starter. Mix to a soft dough using a wooden spoon.

6. Turn the dough out onto a lightly floured surface and knead for 2–3 minutes until smooth. Place in an oiled bowl, cover with cling film and leave to rise for 1–1½ hours or until doubled in size.

7. Turn the dough out and lightly knead again. Return to the bowl, re-cover with oiled cling film and leave in a warm place for about 1 hour or until more than doubled in size (this extra rising gives the bread a light airy texture).

8. Lightly dust two baking sheets with flour. Punch back the dough to deflate, then turn out onto a lightly floured surface. Cut the dough in half and shape each piece into a long oval. Place on the baking sheet, cover with oiled cling film and leave to rise for about 30 minutes.

9. Towards the end of rising time, preheat the oven to 200°C/fan 190°C/400°F/gas 6. Carefully remove the cling film and bake for 25 minutes or until dark golden and hollow-sounding when tapped.

10. Transfer the loaves to a wire rack and leave to cool.

CIABATTA ROLLS

These are the rolls typically used when ordering panini in a café or sandwich shop. Their shape ensures that you can add a generous amount of filling and the light-textured bread remains deliciously soft in the centre when toasted.

Makes 6 x 75g rolls

250g strong white bread flour
1 tsp salt
1 tsp caster sugar
1 tsp fast-action dried yeast
3 tbsp olive oil, plus extra for greasing
175ml lukewarm water

1. Sift the flour, salt and sugar into a large bowl. Stir in the yeast and make a hollow in the middle of the dry ingredients.

2. Pour in 2½ tablespoons of the oil and the water and mix to a soft dough with a wooden spoon. Knead on a lightly floured work surface for 10 minutes, until smooth and elastic.

3. Line an 18 x 28 x 4cm baking tin with baking parchment and generously drizzle with olive oil. Flatten the dough slightly and place in the tin. Let it rest for about 5 minutes, then push and gently stretch the dough out until it is the same size as the tin. Cover with oiled cling film and leave to rise in a warm place until it has more than doubled in size, about 2 hours.

4. Grease a large baking sheet and place on top of the baking tin. Holding both, invert the tin and gently shake the dough onto the baking sheet. Remove the baking parchment.

5. Using a large sharp knife, cut the dough into six rectangles and space them out on the baking sheet. Cover with oiled cling film and leave for about 40 minutes until well risen.

6. Towards the end of rising, preheat the oven to 200°C/fan 190°C/400°F/gas 6.

7. Carefully remove the cling film and bake the rolls for about 20 minutes until they are golden.

8. Remove from the oven, then brush the tops of the hot rolls with the remaining ½ tablespoon oil and leave to cool on the baking sheet.

COOK'S TIPS

When baking rolls for panini making, make sure they are only just cooked or very slightly under-baked, as they will be cooked and browned a bit more on the panini press.

For herb-flavoured rolls, add 1 tablespoon chopped fresh parsley, oregano or basil to the dough, or 1 teaspoon chopped fresh rosemary or thyme or dried mixed herbs.

CUBAN BREAD (PAN CUBANO)

Essential for the classic layered Cuban sandwich, this is a simple white bread with a thin crisp crust and lightly textured centre. It is similar to French bread but often made with ordinary white rather than bread flour and with a much higher proportion of fat, usually lard, which makes it moister and more richly flavoured. A traditional Cuban loaf is very long and far too large to be baked in a conventional oven, so this recipe is for individual Cuban rolls – ideal for making panini.

Makes 6 x 125g rolls

500g plain white flour
4 tsp caster sugar
2 tsp salt
1½ tsp fast-action dried yeast
75g lard or white vegetable fat
300ml lukewarm water

1. Mix the flour, sugar, salt and yeast together in a large bowl. Make a hollow in the middle.

2. Gently melt the lard in a saucepan or in a cling film-covered bowl in the microwave. Pour into the hollow of the dry ingredients, add the water and mix together with a wooden spoon to make a soft dough.

3. Turn out the dough onto a lightly floured surface and knead for 10 minutes until smooth and elastic. Return the mixture to the bowl, cover with cling film and leave to rise in a warm place for about 1 hour, or until doubled in size.

4. Turn out the dough and lightly knead for a few seconds. Divide into six equal pieces. Shape each into a baguette-shaped roll, 16–18cm long. Place on a baking sheet lined with baking parchment and cover with oiled cling film. Leave to rise for about 45 minutes, or until doubled in size.

5. When the loaves are almost fully risen, preheat the oven to 200°C/fan 190°C/400°F/gas 6. Lightly brush the tops with warm water, then cut a shallow lengthways slit down the middle of each.

6. Bake for 10 minutes, then turn down the oven to 180°C/fan 170°C/350°F/ gas 4 and cook for a further 12–15 minutes or until risen and dark golden.

7. Transfer the loaves to a wire cooling rack, cover with a clean tea towel and leave to cool.

BUTTERY BRIOCHE BREAD

Enriched with milk, butter and eggs, this French bread has a wonderful soft texture and is superb when lightly toasted in the panini press. Traditionally it is made in individual moulds and has a fluted bottom and topknot, but when making sandwiches, a loaf-shape is ideal.

Makes a 850g loaf

2 medium eggs
About 175ml milk
450g strong white bread flour
50g caster sugar
1 tsp salt
1¼ tsp fast-action dried yeast
100g butter, at room temperature

1. Grease a 900g loaf tin and line with baking parchment. Whisk the eggs together with a fork in a jug, then add enough milk to reach the 300ml mark. Set aside 1 tablespoon of the mixture for glazing.

2. Sift the flour, sugar and salt into a large bowl. Stir in the yeast, then make a hollow in the middle of the dry ingredients. Pour in the egg and milk mixture and mix to a soft dough using a wooden spoon.

3. Turn out the dough onto a lightly floured work surface and knead for 10 minutes or until smooth and elastic. Grease the

bowl with a little of the butter, add the dough, cover with a tea towel and leave to rise until doubled in size, about 1 hour.

4. Use your hand to incorporate the remaining softened butter into the dough. Turn out onto a lightly floured work surface and knead until the butter is evenly distributed.

5. Shape the dough into a rectangle and place in the prepared tin. Cover with oiled cling film and leave to rise until the dough is nearly at the top of the tin.

6. About 5 minutes before baking, preheat the oven to 200°C/fan 190°C/400°F/gas 6. Lightly brush the top with the reserved egg and milk and bake for 35–40 minutes or until well risen, glossy and golden.

7. Leave in the tin for 5 minutes, then remove and transfer to a wire rack, standing the loaf on its base. Leave to cool.

COOK'S TIPS

For bread-machine brioche, pour the egg and milk mixture into the bread pan. Add the butter and about half of the flour. Add the sugar, then the rest of the flour. Put the salt and yeast in separate corners of the pan. Fit the pan into the bread machine, shut the lid and set to the sweet bread setting with a light crust. Press start button. Remove and cool as main recipe.

To make a chocolate brioche, substitute 25g cocoa powder for 25g of the flour and use light brown sugar instead of caster sugar.

VICTORIAN MILK LOAF

This classic loaf is enriched with semi-skimmed milk and a spoonful of skimmed milk powder. This gives it a soft, almost fluffy, even texture and a lightly floured, golden crust. It works equally well with sweet and savoury panini.

Makes a 750g loaf

600g plus 1 tsp strong white bread flour
4 tsp skimmed milk powder
1½ tsp salt
4 tsp caster sugar
1½ tsp fast-action dried yeast
25g butter
400ml semi-skimmed milk

1. Grease a 900g loaf tin and line with baking parchment. Put the flour, skimmed milk powder, salt, sugar and yeast in a bowl and stir together. Make a hollow in the middle of the dry ingredients.

2. Gently heat the butter in a small saucepan until melted, then turn off the heat and stir in the milk. Pour the buttery milk mixture into the hollow of the dry ingredients and stir together with a wooden spoon to make a soft dough.

3. Turn out the dough onto a lightly floured work surface and knead for 10 minutes until smooth and elastic. Put the dough in a bowl, cover with a clean tea towel and leave to rise until doubled in size, about 1 hour.

4. Knead the dough for a minute, then shape into a rectangle and place in the prepared tin. Cover with oiled cling film and leave to rise until the dough is nearly at the top of the tin.

5. About 5 minutes before baking, preheat the oven to 200°C/fan 190°C/400°F/gas 6. Bake for 35–40 minutes or until well-risen, glossy and golden.

6. Leave in the tin for 2–3 minutes, then remove and transfer to a wire rack, standing the loaf on its base. Lightly dust the top with the remaining flour while the loaf is hot. Leave to cool.

COOK'S TIPS

To make milk loaf in a bread machine, pour the semi-skimmed milk into the pan, then add the butter, followed by the 600g flour. Put the salt, skimmed milk powder and sugar in separate corners of the pan, then make a shallow dip in the middle of the flour and add the yeast. Fit the pan into the bread machine, shut the lid and set to the basic white setting with a light or medium crust. Press start. Remove and cool as main recipe.

Use skimmed milk instead of semi-skimmed if preferred, or full-fat milk (in which case reduce the amount of butter by 5g).

HONEY OATMEAL SODA LOAF

This simple bread can be made in minutes and doesn't require kneading or time to rise; it doesn't include yeast. Oats give it a slightly chewy texture and honey adds a subtle sweetness, making it ideal for both savoury and sweet panini.

Makes an 800g loaf

2 tbsp clear honey
300ml buttermilk
50g porridge oats
225g plain white flour
200g self-rising wholemeal flour
1¼ tsp bicarbonate of soda
¾ tsp salt
25g butter, cut into cubes, plus extra for greasing
1 egg, beaten

1. Mix the honey and buttermilk in a bowl. Stir in the oats, then leave to soak for 30 minutes.

2. Preheat the oven to 200°C/fan 190°C/400°F/gas 6. Grease a 900g loaf tin and line with baking parchment.

3. Sift the flours, bicarbonate of soda and salt into a large bowl, adding the bran left in the sieve. Add the butter and rub in using the tips of your fingers and thumbs, until the mixture looks like fine breadcrumbs. Make a hollow in the middle.

4. Pour the oat mixture into the hollow and mix together with a wooden spoon to make a stiff dough (you may need to use your hands to gently bring the mixture together).

5. Shape the dough into a ball, then into a loaf shape and place in the prepared tin.

6. Bake for 10 minutes, then reduce the temperature to 180°C/fan 170°C/350°F/gas 4 and bake for a further 30 minutes.

7. Leave the bread to cool in the tin for a few minutes, then turn out onto a wire rack and leave to cool completely before slicing.

COOK'S TIPS

When cool, wrap the bread in foil or keep in a plastic bag and use within three days, or freeze for up to a month.

This soda loaf is also good flavoured with cheese. Stir 50g mature grated Cheddar into the mixture after rubbing in the butter in step 3 and before adding the oat mixture.

FLATBREADS

These breads are similar to a pizza dough with a crisp and slightly chewy texture. They are cooked directly on the panini press, so have a smooth or ridged finish depending on your make of panini press.

Makes 2 flatbreads, enough to make 2 sandwiches

250g strong white bread flour
1 tsp salt
1 tsp fast-action dried yeast
2 tbsp olive oil, plus extra for oiling
175ml lukewarm water

1. Sift the flour and salt into a large bowl and stir in the yeast. Make a hollow in the dry ingredients and add the olive oil and water. Mix to a soft, slightly sticky dough using a wooden spoon.

2. Knead the dough on a lightly floured surface for 10 minutes, until smooth and elastic. Try not to add too much flour; it should still be slightly sticky.

3. Place the dough in an oiled bowl, cover with cling film and leave it to rise in a warm place until almost double in size, about 1 hour.

4. Turn out the dough, lightly knead for a minute, then divide into two equal pieces. Loosely cover each with cling film and leave to rest for 10 minutes.

5. Roll out each of the dough pieces to a rectangle about 25 x 20cm; each should be slightly smaller than your panini press, so the size will depend on your model.

6. Heat the panini press according to the manufacturer's instructions.

7. Lift one piece of dough and carefully place it across the bottom half of the press. Pull the top down and cook until pale golden with ridged brown grid marks, 2–4 minutes, depending on how hot your machine is.

8. Carefully remove and repeat with the second piece of dough. Leave the flatbreads to cool.

9. To make panini, place your filling on one flatbread, then top with the other. Return to the panini press and cook. Remove and cut in half to make two portions.

COOK'S TIPS

For cheese flatbread, add 50g grated Parmesan, kneading it into the dough after rising.

For wholewheat flatbread, use half wholewheat and half strong white bread flour and add an extra 1½ tablespoons water when mixing the dough.

INDEX

Panini recipe titles followed by (V) are vegetarian